W0114915

THE
TRUE
AND THE
ETERNAL

LARS MUHL
NALEEA LANDMANN

THE
TRUE
AND THE
ETERNAL

EXPERIENCES WITH THE DIVINE

WATKINS
1893

Avoid the comfortable. Safety is a prison.

Open your heart. Open your wings.

Go where only Angels dare to go. Forget your reputation.

Notice the symphony of harmony. Everywhere.

Let go of control. Don't identify with personality and programming.

All is well in this new moment. Follow your heartbeat.

See behind the apparent. When things become normal, it's time to change.
Everlasting Love. As below, so above.

Never say 'never' or 'I can't do that'. You are pure Compassionate Consciousness.

Kindness brings peace. Be patient.

Allow it to manifest and be free.

Now fly into eternity.

"The true science of words and sounds has been lost, but not irretrievably so. In the ages to come it will be recovered once again, creating thereby a greater union and harmony between heaven and earth, between the Angels and humanity, and between all the nations and peoples of the world. The Holy Tongue, lost and forgotten, will be spoken again in all its purity, and the prophecies found in the sacred scriptures will be fulfilled." (*The Book of Light* – Sefer ha-Zohar, as quoted in SENSA by Dorje Jinpa)

"Unless you come to yourselves and become like children again, you will not enter the Kingdom of Heaven. He who humbles himself and becomes like this child is the greatest in the Kingdom of Heaven." (*Gospel of Matthew* 18:3–4)

"There seems to be a barrier between the visible and the invisible, that separates us, but this is not true; there is no barrier except in your own minds, there alone exists the barrier between us. Then get rid of this barrier, this separation, through understanding and Love." (Murdo MacDonald-Bayne)
"The intuitive mind is a sacred gift, and the rational mind is a faithful servant. We have created a society that honours the servant and has forgotten the gift." (Albert Einstein)

"You yourself are the abyss that opens below you as well as the bridge you must cross. You are the path you must follow and the mountain you must climb. You are the inner space you must find and take possession of. And when you rest there, you will realize that you are the cloud that floats in the sky, that you are the rain that falls and evaporates again; that you are the drop that will soon become an ocean. Then you will know God." (*The Θ Manuscript*)

"A heavenly attitude is theirs, those whose love is without condition; they will, therefore, receive unconditional love." (*Gospel of Matthew* 5:3–11)

The True and The Eternal
Lars Muhl
Naleea Landmann

First published in the UK and USA in 2025 by
Watkins, an imprint of Watkins Media Limited
Unit 11, Shepperton House, 83–89 Shepperton Road
London N1 3DF

enquiries@watkinspublishing.com

A CIP record for this book is available from the British Library

ISBN: 978-1-83681-000-1 (Hardback)
ISBN: 9978-1-83681-001-8 (eBook)

10 9 8 7 6 5 4 3 2 1

Printed and bound by CPI Group (UK) Ltd, Croydon, CR0 4YY

www.watkinspublishing.com

The manufacturer's authorised representative in the EU
for product safety is eucomply OÜ - Pärnu mnt 139b-14,
11317 Tallinn, Estonia, hello@eucompliancepartner.com,
www.eucompliancepartner.com

MIX
Paper | Supporting
responsible forestry
FSC® C171272

CONTENTS

EPHATAH

In the presence of the open heavens

We are many. Many who deeply care, whose innermost wish is that we live in peace and kindness, community, companionship and freedom.

May this book provide both information and frequencies, memories and visions, downloads and inspirations to all who are here to walk the path of harmony and unity – the path that has been present beyond all opposites at all times and under all circumstances, waiting to be noticed, acknowledged and explored. It is the path of spirit and soul, of inner guidance and vision, power and realization – the path of love without conditions and without exceptions.

These pages are written for all who long to live by the essence of their true being and their soul's calling. For all who remember how to enter into the eternal now, even if they tend to forget it when the waves of our everyday lives are crashing high. For all who care. For all who worry about and suffer from the manifold manifestations of our perception of duality. For all who know – always have, always will. For all who have not found their true place upon the sacred lands of this beautiful planet where we came together to live in brother and sisterhood. For all who arrived with trust and certainty and are now saddened, bewildered and discouraged. For all who change the world every day through a smile or a helping hand. For the healers and dancers, the revolutionaries and caretakers, the dreamers and poets, the tender and the silent ones, the wise and the wild, the trusting and the kind ones. We are many.

Who are we without our logic, our scientific findings, our beliefs, traditions, sentiments and preferences, pains and traumas? Can we trust that there is something else to be found beyond those well-known comrades? How will our lives be if we dare to let go of all our identifications? What landscapes will we enter in our hearts and minds?

Who will we be? Who will this "I" be, that is me – and this "I" that is you? Will we be able to hear and follow our inner guidance when we leave existence and enter reality? Will we still live "in the world"? Will we have a place there? Or will we find something beyond this world? How will life be when we remember our true being, our heritage and our home?

Our heart can gather all our questions as if they were stars that have fallen from the sky right into our very being. They will start to shine and sparkle in us, becoming precious inspirations instead of burdens that feel heavy on our minds and shoulders.

May the wisdom that dwells in the depths of our hearts guide us, may the power of our spirit embrace us and may the presence of our soul shine through us wherever we go.

Naleea Landmann

GRATITUDE TO THE DIVINE FEMININE

We abide side by side

In my life, the tender and wild, nurturing and provoking, all-accepting and uncompromising, inspiring and challenging, healing and transforming power of the Divine Feminine has been an absolute presence in everything I have done. My creativity has always been ignited and raised by this power that I have experienced through the women I have developed a deep bond of friendship or had an intimate relationship with. Therefore, I would like to express my deepest gratitude to these women.

First and foremost, to my mother Alice for her friendship and for showing me what it means to take responsibility for what matters in life and for always trusting me.

Thanks to my little sister Lone, a master of masters, who within a lifespan of only seven years showed me what unconditional trust and love really means.

Thanks to my spiritual Guides and Guarding Angels Ishatar, Miriam, Zoé and Taxo for always being present.

Thanks Hanne, for showing me the Earth, the cats, the birds, the trees and the flowers, the skies and the waters, the secret islands and the freedom that roams there.

Thanks Irene Ba-Bé, for entering my life at a time when I most needed your wild wisdom and the travels we did together.

Thanks Githa, for everything you have given and the love

we shared. Thanks for all we experienced together, for the songs and music and the teachings we created. Thanks for your beautiful and genuine voice of freedom. Thanks for the many travels to Israel, where both of us seemed to flourish, exploring our ancient spiritual heritage.

Thanks Kirsten P, Tinne S, Kristina J, Kristina T, Ana S, Karen M, Ingeborg, Helle H and Sus K, for your unconditional friendship.

Thanks Pia R for your precious voice, and for connecting me to the Seer Calle Montségur, and Ulla R for keeping me in touch with him after he left this world.

Thanks Sylvia for your insights into the Divine Feminine, without which my book *The Grail* wouldn't have been written.

Thanks Carol C, for your readings and keeping me focused on my purpose in this incarnation.

Thanks Naleea, for bringing clarity into my life and work, for being such a huge inspiration by your seriousness and integrity, who never needs to make a fuss about the miracles you perform in everyday life. Thanks for everything you have brought to the books *The Light Within a Human Heart*, *The Sacred Numbers of Initiation* and *The God Formula*, and for your translation of them. Thanks for your graceful voice of truth and compassion. Thanks for adding your words and wisdom to my inspirations in this present book. You are truly the clarifier, balancer and protector. And here is a golden astrology legend that underlines the kinship in our work:

"Scorpio, in its lowest aspect, represents the Tree of Knowledge (intellect and science). When Scorpio is able to elevate itself to a higher plane of realization, it transforms into an Eagle, representing the Tree of Life (God Consciousness). Libra was the last sign of the twelve to be discovered and is the least visible in the sky. Libra balances everything and its highest calling is to balance Scorpio with the Eagle, thereby protecting the Tree of Life (God Consciousness)."

Lars Muhl

1

ENTRANCE INTO THE MYSTERY

Listening to the power that opens a flower

This book is an attempt to describe a series of personal experiences that are in many ways indescribable and perhaps incomprehensible. Indescribable because they are spiritual in nature, and incomprehensible because spirit is not a recognized factor in a world where humanity is faced with incalculable problems that have been created precisely because we are unaware of what a human being really is and what metaphysical abilities we possess. The aim of the book is to draw the reader's attention to these abilities, which are always available to us – and always have been.

The book is about God Consciousness! God? So, is it a religious book?

No, not in the conventional sense. Instead, the book gives a new description of what God is and what consequences an understanding and awareness about the presence of our spiritual heritage has for human life right now.

God is pure consciousness. As the father of quantum physics Max Planck said: "Behind all creation there is an intelligent force." This force is the consciousness we are talking about. An intelligent force far beyond our intellectual reach – all-harmonious, all-encompassing, unrestricted, unconditional, unchallengeable, absolute, almighty, complete.

This book is about that consciousness, which has been called many names in many different traditions. We will not focus on beliefs or theories, but on experiences. Our experiences in this life and other lifetimes, and those of others that have helped and inspired us on our life's journey.

If there are passages that seem incomprehensible, please don't discard the whole book. We ask for your patience, dear reader. Please, take the time to read them again.

Spiritual science is the oldest science in human history. It differs from natural science in the focus of its research, which leads to a completely different field of knowledge. In spiritual science, experimental insight has always been gained through inner perception and reflection instead of outer observation and suggestion. It is the Path of the Mystic. The path of everyone who includes the awareness of our inner realms in their everyday experience.

It is our hope that this book will draw the reader's attention to what a human being is; that we are more than just body and mind and the ability to think, sense and feel; that we are first and foremost spirit – a fact that, when understood, is the one and only missing piece in the puzzle that can keep humanity from the continuation of the path of oblivion and destruction that we took.

When a patient is sick, we always try to find a diagnosis before we know what cure to apply. This book points to a cure that heals all diseases and any kind of imbalance, no matter the specific diagnosis.

The consciousness that is described in this book is not a new discovery. Many mystics have talked about it, many artists have been inspired by it, and many people have been healed by it. Once we become aware of this consciousness, we will find it everywhere: in the blood of every living being, in every cell of our body, in the air we breathe, under the soles of our feet, in the chamber of our heart, in the fabric of our mind, even in the most hardened creature. It connects us to all life, all expressions of life, to every cycle, from the smallest flower in the meadow to the outermost galaxy in the most distant universe.

Yet few people know about it, take it seriously or consciously live in accordance with it. That is why it is important that information about its existence is written down, so that those who one day find themselves at a dead end or at a crossroads not knowing which way to go, realize that the truth they sought externally is the gift that humanity was endowed with internally when we were created. We *are* this consciousness. All of it, not just parts of it. We *are it*, and all the qualities that belong to it. We *are* the intelligent force, and we are expressing it in our own personalized way, just like every flower expresses itself in its own unique way. The discovery of that gift has always been and always will be the absolute prerequisite for any real personal or collective breakthrough, development and transformation.

All the qualities we normally attribute to the few men and women who today are considered true saints, avatars and prophets, are both expressions of and vessels for this gift within each one of us. These qualities, like presence, patience, loving kindness, gratitude and gracefulness are waiting to be discovered in us, like seeds waiting to grow once we are ready to water them. Those men and women who expressed the divine frequencies of omnipotence, omniscience and omnipresence and lived their lives by them did not come here to receive any personal gain, but to stand by us throughout our life's journey as wisdom keepers, visionaries and healers, to open us to a wider understanding of reality and to show us the way to the Higher Consciousness that is anchored in all of us. They knew that their task would only succeed by inspiring us through their own example.

Now the question is whether this consciousness is a gift we want to accept and integrate into our cognitive awareness or whether it is just a disturbing element in our current life with all its strategies and norms, perceptions and opinions about what life is and what it is not, and what role we are called to play in it.

Perhaps you have already found your place? But if not – if you read what we have to share with you and take it to heart, the consequences will most likely be life-changing, as the words express a reality and a path that stands in stark contrast to almost everything that humankind today perceives as real and true.

We all have a choice. The choice is between presence or absence, sincerity or superficiality, true or false, life or death. In reality, there is no middle ground. You cannot be just a little bit pregnant or just a little bit true. Either you are or you are not. True to what? To your own perception, your own inspiration, your own inner voice, your dreams, your visions, your very being – that *something* in you that will arise beyond the loudness and chores of everyday life, and that is expressing who you really are if you let it be part of your conscious awareness. So, either you are true to your inner Self, which is the gift we are talking about, or not. And consequently, we also have the situation of a choice when we are faced with finding a new path at the end of a blind alley, when we are confronted with sickness that needs to be healed, when we experience a falling that calls for a rebirth and when we allow the hidden to be revealed. For that to happen, we must know who we truly are, where we come from, what we are doing here and where we are going. We must know the gift that we have all been given and that this book will try to describe.

We are not following any particular religion. Yet we have been drawn to the essence and path of all religions for a lifetime. The vast majority of us humans on this planet are, at least culturally, affiliated with one of the five major faiths, Hinduism, Buddhism, Judaism, Christianity or Islam. Most people in the Western world have grown up in a Christian tradition and culture, have been baptized and confirmed, without this apparently resulting in anything more than a superficial knowledge of the actual message of Christianity or its main scripture, the Bible, with its Old and New Testaments. Many people consider the book to be incomprehensible and therefore irrelevant to them.

Let's clarify what the term *religion* stands for. It comes from the Latin *re-ligare*, which translates to re-connect, re-bind[1] and re-new. This means that the true purpose of a religion is to establish a field of belonging, as well as to reconnect its followers with something they once had a bond or relation with, but now seem to have forgotten. In other words, we must assume that religion was meant to be our tool to reconnect to God Consciousness.

It seems that this reconnection has only happened on a superficial level until now, which must be attributed to the long line of Church fathers and theologians who, from the beginning of Christianity to the present day, projected and explained the divine principles behind a faith that has slowly but surely drifted so far apart from its own head, Yeshua the Nazarene (Jesus Christ),[2] in such a way, that – just as in Fyodor Dostoyevsky's novel *The Brothers Karamazov* – today he would not recognize the movement that was created in his name 2,000 years ago.

The Grand Inquisitor hurls accusations at Yeshua in the novel after he has him arrested: "You wanted to make mankind free, but you did not understand mankind and did not understand that if there is one thing mankind cannot tolerate, it is freedom. We, your church, on the other hand, have understood this. People love comfort more than freedom. Only when they have reliable guardians to guide them through life do they feel safe. We have improved your

---

[1]   The word for *truth* in Aramaic (*sharara/sherara/serara*) means to be tightly bound together, like strings of fabric that then form a rope.

[2]   In Aramaic, the language Jesus spoke, he is called Yeshua. Jesus is a Romanized version of the original name Yeshua. "Christos" is Greek and means "the Anointed One", just like the Aramaic/Hebrew "Messiah".

work. Isn't that the work of love toward mankind? Why have you come again? Why do you want to disturb our work?"

Yeshua remains silent during the cardinal's outburst of anger. Then he gets up and walks over to the Grand Inquisitor and kisses him on the mouth. The kiss burns the old man's heart and he instinctively realizes that he is standing in front of something that is bigger than anything else he has ever encountered before. He is faced with a choice he must make, the choice between the reality of Yeshua or the illusion on which he has built his life's work. The Grand Inquisitor chooses the latter, opens the cell door and shouts, "Go, and never come back – never!"

We have distorted the formless by creating a form and turned our backs on the content. Yeshua and his teachings of unconditional love and compassion are simply too radical. His wisdom seems to disrupt all our strategies in the marketplace we call "the real world", in which everything is for sale and anyone can be bought. The definition and experience of our love has been reduced to include exclusively that or those who serve our needs. It only embraces those who declare that they love us, thereby helping to maintain our self-image. We have yet to grasp that true love equals honesty. That love is not a grocery store where I love you if you love me.

In my work, I have met people of all kinds from all walks of life. Time and time again, I have seen that the suffering that sends people to me is entirely due to the decisions – or lack thereof – that we each make or fail to make, not only in this life but just as much in previous incarnations. The same is true in my own life. I too must constantly grapple with the consequences of past decisions and actions. But the insights gained from my spiritual experiences guide me through the grief and suffering, and open doors that were previously hermetically sealed to the healing essence of life, revealing the hidden, raising the fallen and healing the broken. There is only one way to deal with past mistakes and that is to face them and change your attitude and behaviour now.

The vast majority of suffering is caused by the belief that physical existence is the only existence, and that death is the absolute end of life. This way of perceiving life results in an underlying, very often unconscious feeling of fundamental meaninglessness that is reflected in virtually everything people do and experience. And from this meaninglessness comes an equally fundamental alienation and anxiety that manifests itself in restless and neurotic behaviour, resulting in a host of mental and physical disorders. It's a vicious and seemingly unbreakable circle, being trapped in the hamster wheel of hopelessness or complacency. But there is one question that will get us out of our corner of captivity. That question is: what are we really doing here, what is our purpose?

In our time and our cultural and customary landscape, the idea of reincarnation is not widely accepted or understood. But in the pre-Christian era in the Middle East, as well as in the ancient Chinese, Native American, Indian, Persian, Egyptian, Greek and Jewish mystery traditions, reincarnation was and is not an expression of wishful or ephemeral thinking but was viewed matter-of-factly as a natural part of life: humans have only one life – and that life is eternal.

One life, but many lifetimes. We choose a role, a script and a costume, enter the stage of life and play our part. When the play is over, we leave the stage, step into the wings and reflect on the mystery of life and what we have just experienced until we are ready to take on a new costume and a new script and step on and off the stage of life again and again and again. But not necessarily here on Earth. Life unfolds everywhere in all the universes of infinity. We all incarnate where we can have the most meaningful experiences and where what we each have to give is most needed.

If we want to reach higher realizations through spiritual work, we eventually find out that religions and other spiritual traditions will always be some kind of artificial aid, a worn-out crutch or a temporary substitute for a God or the Nirvana that, according to religions, is beyond humanity's fallen nature and can only be reached and earned through membership and submission. But as Mahatma Gandhi said: "God has no religion."

Does this mean that religions have no role or value for our lives today? That must be an individual question. If you're looking for fellowship, you will very often meet many helping hands and valuable social structures in religious communities. Sometimes though, the belonging and shelter we receive in certain communities need to be paid for with the price of conformity – or exclusion in the case of those who are unwilling to follow the direction of the majority.

But if you want to tap into the power that this book is about, you must be able to rest within yourself. This means being able to stand alone, even being cut off from contact with other people – at least for a time. To let new thoughts and qualities develop within you. Seek silence. Feel who you are. Then you will be a stronger vessel for the gifts you have come here to share in any form of co-operation and interaction with others.

Does this mean that you don't need help or shouldn't ask for it when you feel that a problem seems to be too huge for you? That you should not work with a therapist or a teacher when you want to explore your inner, spiritual life and perhaps begin a spiritual practice? Again, it's an individual matter. Stay open to what comes to you, after you have acknowledged that you need help, inspiration or companionship. From then on, anyone we meet on our path must be considered to be the teacher we need right now. Maybe you'll hear about a therapist from a friend, a book will be given to you or you will receive an answer in your meditation.

Being able to stand alone is not synonymous with loneliness. It has become almost a dogma or widespread misconception that the celebrity with thousands of followers is less lonely than someone who is unknown and has no "friends". Such dogma is just another example of the superficiality that characterizes our times. No matter how many new photos of ourselves we post, it doesn't dissolve the inner restlessness that desperately seeks other people's recognition. Therefore, we must ask ourselves how it is that we have completely lost confidence in ourselves to such an extent that we must constantly receive confirmation from others that we are lovable and good enough.

Again and again, we must be willing to face our personalities and ask ourselves, what motivates our thoughts, words and actions. Why do we do what we do? Sometimes we realize that everything needs to be reviewed and renewed. This is the process Yeshua talks about in the New Testament when he tells us that we must be reborn in this life before we can truly enter the Kingdom of Heaven.[3] A process that may have to be repeated several times in life.

But what is the Kingdom of Heaven that Yeshua is talking about? Where is it located? What does it contain? According to Yeshua, the Kingdom of Heaven is our only true inner and outer reality,[4] the reality of the All-Harmonious. It is always accessible to us, yet we disregard and discard its presence in uncountable ways. Our intellect collects the reasoning against such a ground-breaking view of reality, and our hearts and psyche are shouting for "proof, proof!", before they allow themselves to leave the seemingly secure positions of former beliefs and life experiences and dedicate and surrender themselves to set foot on such a life-changing path.

"The Kingdom of Heaven is within you – and all around you."

Being reborn means the state we enter in the moment we make a decision to leave a disharmonious attitude, a behaviour, a thought or an emotion behind, and dedicate ourselves to integrate and follow the Law of Light in our lives. The Law of Light is a vibrational field of eternal harmony and

---

[3]   *Gospel of John* 3:21

[4]   *Gospel of Luke* 17:21 and *Gospel of Thomas* 3

grace that is expressing itself through us via unconditional peacefulness, love and compassion. It is a sacred mirror that reflects our true image as children of God to us if we have not blurred or stained it through ignoring its essence, the Golden Rule: do not do to others what you don't want done to you. Remembering to polish this mirror every evening before we go to sleep, for example, is a deeply transformative practice. At what time throughout our day did we stain it, and why? What did we think we would gain by leaving the frequency of kindness and care? Being right? Being first? Or where did we leave the frequency of trust? Believing we could not do something or feeling not worthy in some way? Worthy of what? We are children of God, each one of us, we never need to prove ourselves – we only need to live according to the truth we know so well in our hearts. Caring for our pains as much as for the pains of the others, yet, first and foremost, filling our lives and our bodies with the divine presence: with kindness, joy, care, vitality, generosity and peacefulness. Becoming deliverers, providers and beacons of those divinely human qualities.

What is it that governs our lives? For the majority of us, it seems that our emotions have taken over. One moment we are happy, the next we are deeply unhappy. Emotions are very powerful. They determine how we perceive the world and how we see other people. The problem is that our attitude toward another person or situation can change in seconds. It is therefore reasonable to ask ourselves the question, is it even possible to trust what we feel, see and perceive as real?

The fact that we humans are capable of expressing emotions, showing compassion and empathizing with other living beings is what defines us as a species. We, who are so sure that we are the crown of life's great creation simply because we have managed to put some wires together and create a technological development that – when it comes down to it, and in relation to the God Consciousness we are talking about – is no more sophisticated than when the first humans discovered how to create fire by rubbing a piece of wood against a stone. We measure and we weigh, we count and compile statistics, but we are not even close to solving the mystery of life itself. What the naked eye cannot see and the physical ear cannot hear does not exist in our world. Testimonies from people who have consciously travelled through the tunnel of death or have been lifted into other realms through a spiritual experience and met deceased family members and Beings of Light in the form of Siddhartha (the Buddha) and Yeshua/Jesus at the end of the tunnel, are refuted as phenomena caused by chemical short circuits in the witnesses' brains.

The fact that many, after being in deep states of coma – some even after having experienced a shutdown of major parts of their brain activity[5] – still come back to life and give detailed accounts of existence on the other side of death, has led the way to more and more people sharing their life-changing accounts of near-death or out-of-body experiences. We are about to shake those once rock-hard belief systems like "what cannot be explained simply does not exist".

History is full of stories that testify that our reality is far more complex and wonderful than we make it out to be. Have we forgotten all the mysteries? The Oriental and Greek mystics? The Chinese Taoists, the Celtic Sages, the Mongolian Shamans, the Wisdom Keepers of the Native American Tribes, the Māori Elders, the Hawaiian Healers? We, who think we are so advanced and evolved, need to ask ourselves what happened to our knowledge and understanding about our great cosmic and spiritual heritage? Have we traded it all away for digital and electrical gadgets and artificial intelligence? An intelligence which, when it comes down to it, is only a limited and poor imitation of the wisdom of the Spirit within each one of us.

---

[5]   Eben Alexander: *Proof of Heaven: A Neurosurgeon's Journey into the Aterlife.*

I come from a non-religious family. We hardly ever went to church and didn't talk about faith, Jesus, the Holy Spirit or God. The religion lessons at school didn't teach me much, only that I couldn't reconcile myself with the interpretations of the Bible that were part of the teachers' curriculums. It wasn't because I had read the Bible myself at the time, it was just a certainty in me that I did not doubt. The depiction of a punishing and judgemental God was not only incomprehensible to me, but also made me almost embarrassed for the teacher. Yet my life has been one long orientation toward God and the Divine. And I am talking of a different image of God than the old white bearded man sitting on his throne, judging humankind as favourable and unfavourable people or tribes. The question is how we each define God. It could be helpful to gain a new understanding of the concepts we use today to express faith and spirituality. An understanding derived from spiritual experience rather than theological dogma and secular speculation.

It is often the miracles mentioned in the New Testament that divide the waters and cause offence. Many consider Jesus to be a myth invented by the Church, and nothing more, because the miracles go against all accepted reason that is based 100 per cent on "natural science" with its entirely pragmatic and materialistic way of thinking. Nowadays, natural science has actually become a new form of religion.

If only it was understood that the so-called "Jesus miracles" are not a break with the laws of nature but rather a breakthrough to a more extensive human potential and a new and expanded comprehension of the reality we find ourselves in. A potential and a reality that has been completely displaced by a raw, materialistic approach to life and the world. But how was it possible that only a few mystics within the Christian church openly communicated this fact? Because the Church evolved first and foremost into a power apparatus that was more concerned with worldly goods than living the standards and teachings it preached.

At the same time, the true teachings of Jesus were supplanted and replaced with half-truths and often inexplicable theologies. When you realize that the transcendent element of quantum physics stems directly from esoteric mysticism as expressed in the great world religions and spiritual traditions, you will understand that true religion has nothing to do with damnation, hell, abuse and megalomaniac gurus. Esoteric mysticism is an ancient, eternally reviving, metaphorical and symbolic language that must be acknowledged and understood before we are able to find the hidden treasures in the sacred scriptures, such as certain books in the Bible, the Vedas, etcetera. But it is also a continually evolving and expanding language developed by the lessons learned on our path toward Higher Consciousness.

It is through integrating the wisdom of mysticism and spiritual science that we will receive solutions to the problems that humanity has created for itself, so how can we make this integration a main focus in our lives and our social structures? If we don't know what a human being is and what opportunities we have been given, the problems will only accumulate. Today, there are all kinds of opinions about religion. But how can we have an opinion about anything if we've only read or heard about it and haven't had any experiences to support our opinion? And when we have experienced and cannot find words for what we have experienced, we must search until we find. And the very fact that we don't give up or settle for half solutions opens up a whole new frequency in the consciousness that this book is about.

I am fully aware that untold many people over the years have had deeply afflicted experiences with members of the Church institutions as well as various spiritual sects, and that these memories or reports only reinforce the prevalent resistance to investigate religion and spirituality further. There are countless examples of unbearable attacks on children by priests and nuns under the shielding cloak of the

Catholic Church. Add to these heart-wrenching crimes the countless examples of self-appointed gurus, seducing a large or small group of gullible people, often ending tragically for those involved.

When I think about how selfish needs and ego-gratifications, the eternal pursuit of comfort, coupled with fear, greed, materialism and ignorance rule almost every thing, and how easy it would be to activate the spiritual power we all carry within us that would once and for all correct our problems and enable us to create a completely new and far more meaningful life, I know it is time to describe this power, how it works and how to activate it NOW!

In my understanding and experience of the world, nothing is random. Everything is connected, we are all connected, and everything we send out returns to us sooner or later. In this way, we ourselves create the reality we continuously find ourselves in. For example, it's no coincidence to me that most people in the West are raised in a Christian environment. When we are baptized and confirmed in Christianity, it has a deeper meaning, just like everything else we decide to be a part of. We will do ourselves and the world a great favour by opening ourselves to this greatly undiscovered reality of our human existence, listening more seriously and looking deeper into this mystery. Nothing is easier than writing off everything we don't know or understand. All it takes to open the door to the mystery is our total presence. In everything, all the time, everywhere. That sounds daunting? Yes, for sure. But at the same time, this understanding is the biggest relief we can find, because it brings us total freedom and empowerment.

Everywhere people are being talked down to. In the media, from politicians, on TV and in the vast majority of the entertainment industry. We have moved so far away from the ways of old, when leaders were civil servants of the people and their lands, and rules and laws were not based on paving the way for the survival of the cleverest. The citizens are reduced to consumers, voting cattle, the elderly burden, cannon fodder, etcetera. Social media and computer games offer spaces of emotional release and distraction that turn into prisons if screen time is filling up the largest part of our days and nights. Social environments begin to be challenging and basic social skills are either not considered relevant or have not been passed on.

The result is ultimately creating generations that are – on top of not being connected with an awareness of the spiritual dimension of life – socially incapable and suffering from an increase of feelings and diagnoses of anxiety and isolation. That's why it's more important than ever that we wake up from this technocratic nightmare that keeps us in a state of passive allowance, of being led into a future of isolation and de-humanization and start taking care and responsibility for our own lives. Only then can we do something epochal and positive for ourselves and at the same time for all others. Because the potential we humans are carrying inside of us holds the image of a whole new human being – living in harmony and balance with ourselves, other people, all tribes and nations, the lands and seas and the entire plant and animal kingdoms of our planet. Our beautiful planet, the Earth, that we have called Mother Earth, and that we have the privilege to inhabit.

2

ANOTHER TIME, ANOTHER PLACE

And suddenly there was eternity

From the moment I was able to read, I have always been fascinated by gaining insight into other people's experiences. It was as if, on a subconscious level, I knew that having, making and sharing experiences is one of the main reasons why we are incarnated here on Earth, the implication being we are here to learn and to expand our consciousness.

I wasn't very old before I started thinking about where we humans really come from. My mother told me in her late years how, when I was about six years old, I had expressed my astonishment at how primitive the world is. I remember always observing people, wondering why they spoke or acted the way they did. How was it possible that people were so different to that what I perceived as "real"? I felt very close to my parents, but at the same time I never truly felt understood. Did other children have the same experiences? Despite many physical similarities, I somehow felt completely different to my parents and the rest of my family. For example, no one in my family showed the slightest signs of musicality. I felt I had to adapt to a surrounding that did not seem truly recognizable to me. Later I realized that it is the experiences, not only from this life, but from countless incarnations, that define a human being.

I understood that anyone can say and claim anything, and that this is mostly customary everywhere and is an accepted strategy for people to achieve this or that. Similarly, if we were able to realize and accept the consequences of the noise and obscurity, the mental and emotional impact on others and ourselves left by any kind of lie, the world would look very different from how it does now and has done for thousands of years. And it's sort of there, in that realization, that my current life began.

I was born on 14 November 1950 in Aarhus, Denmark on Vestre Ringgade 168. Does that matter? Yes, it does. The time and place of our arrival in physical reality indicates a point and leaves a mark in the ether, specifically in the Book of Life, where all human events, doings and experiences are recorded. Through this point it is subsequently possible for anyone to read information about a particular soul.

My earliest memory is of soft Light flickering around me. The Light is simultaneously powerful and vital, but suddenly I have the feeling of being pulled back from it into a world of shadows, like when a theatre curtain is closing and the stage lights dim. In the world of shadows, the sun shines, the rain falls, the wind blows, something goes up, something goes down, there is good and evil, heat and cold, happiness and sadness, honesty and lies, and I realize that this is the world as it is for most people.

My mother, Alice Burkal Muhl, was a hairdresser with her own salon in our apartment, my father Poul Muhl Pedersen was, like his father Karl Pedersen before him, a taxi driver. Later, when my mother sold the salon, she became manager of the jewellery department in the Salling department store, while my father got a job at the Ceres breweries. My parents gave us children a perfect childhood in every way. Though they didn't understand everything that happened to me later on, they would always allow me my freedom because they basically trusted me. As my mother stated in a radio interview, when asked if she was worried about me after my band Daisy was jailed in Israel in 1969: "Absolutely not, I know that he will be able to take care of himself."

My mum was the solid anchor of the family, while my dad was more unreliable and, some would say, verging on irresponsible. He was a passionate gambler. The problem was that he didn't have the kind of money it takes to be a big player. As a result, we occasionally found our home being hoovered out of furniture because the bailiff had paid a visit. But my father was a generous man, and even though my mother was often frustrated by being constantly challenged existentially, she loved him unconditionally. He retained an eternal street-boy charisma until his death, and she often expressed how much she missed him after he had gone.

From my earliest childhood, I have felt a close connection to all living things – especially people, animals or plants that weren't treated right. It was said that I possessed a high sense of justice, which thus also included trees. I was not very old when, on one December evening, in the run-up to Christmas – while my mum was working late in the salon – I brought the Christmas tree in from the balcony, where it had been left to wait and last until Christmas Eve.

My mum later found it in my bed, where I lay hugging it. After all, it shouldn't be out there alone in the cold, being cut off from its roots. This episode became a story that was told over and over again in my family, the bottom line being that I would have been looking so much forward to the upcoming Christmas days that I even wanted to sleep next to the tree. No matter how often I tried to explain the real reason, they just laughed, leaving me angry and hurt. Not so much because the adults laughed, but because for some reason they didn't want to understand my compassionate motives, which they thought were just the naïve imaginings of a child. In their reality, a felled tree was a dead tree. They had no awareness or connection to its spirit or to the beings that were living on it. But when adults call children naïve in such cases, it is actually they who are the naïve ones.

In our neighbourhood lived a woman who was born with dwarfism, Miss Henriksen. I always felt very shy around her. Sometimes, images of her appeared in my mind and I became overwhelmed with fear that I would stop growing myself one day. How would my life be, I wondered? And how does she feel, day in and out? I felt her loneliness, which made my heart feel lonely too. I remember asking my mum for money a couple of times, which I then ran over and put into Miss Henriksen's hands as soon as I saw her on the street. She looked quite puzzled but, before she could refuse, I was already long gone. Only much later did I realize how embarrassing it must have been for her. Or maybe not. Maybe she did feel my wholehearted wish to somehow show her that she was not alone. Looking back, I feel like talking to myself at that age, and letting him see and experience the countless other ways he could have expressed his care, besides through giving her money.

My little sister, Lone Burkal Pedersen, was born on 6 April 1954 when I was four years old. She had my father's features, big brown eyes and a dark complexion. I had my mum's blue eyes and delicate skin. Despite these traits, my sister was the light one while I was the dark. People were drawn to her like planets orbiting a sun. I was the introverted witness.

When she was about two or three years old, she would wait every night until I had fallen asleep before she got up from her bed and gathered all my clothes that I had left behind, scattered all over the room, and put them in perfect order so I wouldn't get a scolding for my slackness.

I had started first grade at Samsøgades Elementary School when I was five, but felt so alienated there, that the only thing that kept me going were the little writings, which initially only consisted of the words I was able to spell. I remember a clear feeling, that words and writings were somehow going to be an important part of what I was going to do in life. When I had written something, Lone was my enthusiastic audience and she applauded me every time I had read aloud a new story to her. I don't remember exactly what my stories and narratives were about, only that I felt that writing and storytelling itself was vital and essential. She saw a Light in me. When I got a toy car, she got the box it had been in. When I brought the car with me wherever I went, she brought the box and was always beaming with happiness and gratitude. She never asked for anything but was so excited on my behalf, that she would jump and dance around in joy.

She was four years old the first time our father brought her to Marselisborg Hospital because the doctor thought that the skin irritations she had been suffering from for a while could be serious. On her very first day at the hospital, she registered how the nurses rolled up gauze. Every time we visited her after that, she was busy rolling gauze and the nurses told us that she insisted on doing it all day and that no one could do it better than her. She was hospitalized for a couple of weeks before being sent home with no explanation of what was wrong with her.

It was a sunny Sunday morning at six o'clock while our parents were still asleep. My sister and I were playing cobbler in the living room. It was a game we both enjoyed and inexplicably connected us in an activity that I later felt had something to do with a shared past life. All the family shoes were lined up in a row as we took pair after pair, polished them, changed worn laces and "repaired" them. The sun sent its first rays into the living room. Suddenly, in a flash, a veil was removed from the world of solid things. As if reality had turned itself inside out. In that moment I clearly saw the structure and very essence of all the things around me, a web of tiny Light particles connected by thin, pulsating threads of brilliant Light that seemed to continue into eternity. I saw right through our furniture, through the walls and through my sister – everything, my sister included, seemed to be held together by this vibrating web. Then, the opening closed and the veil was back again. It all happened so quickly but also so clearly and precisely that I had no doubt what I had just witnessed was a different and greater reality than the one we normally identify with. I knew that this had to be God's world. Not the God I heard about in religion lessons at school and didn't understand or couldn't relate to. But I was sure there was another God, although I wasn't able to find any words or explanations at the time. I just knew! And it is this inexplicable certainty that has always been with me and that I now know is found in all people.

From then on, a change occurred. I withdrew. The physical world suddenly seemed a dangerous place. It appeared that no one was aware of what they were doing. This feeling was not helped by the fact that my sister's condition worsened.

Once again, she was hospitalized. After many tests, the doctors found that she had a brain tumour and that surgery was required. But it would not be an easy operation. Her chances of survival were fifty-fifty.

Older boys from the ward in the hospital wrote her love letters. The doctors formed a band, drumming on bedpans and boxes and singing nursery rhymes as they circled her bed. She was a Light in the midst of darkness and despair.

She had been in hospital for a month, and it was close to her sixth birthday. As this day was extra special, my mum and dad wanted to give her the bike she had wanted so badly. Our parents were definitely not wealthy, and they had to borrow money to buy a new bike.

When we brought it to my sister into the hospital, she smiled both sadly and encouragingly when she saw it. Then she asked my parents to return it to the shop, "I won't be needing it anyway," she said matter-of-factly. And I have to add that all this was completely devoid of drama or sentimentality from her side. Instead, there was a luminous clarity around her.

Is it even possible to understand such a sentence spoken by a six-year-old girl who knows she is going to die soon? That remark shook our parents to such an extent that they couldn't find anything to say in reply. My sister didn't want them to waste their money on something that could never be used. At the time, the doctors had performed certain procedures that meant she had her entire head bound and was squinting in one eye. But she never complained. Not once. It still moves me today when I think about the state she was in. Was it in spite of, or was it really because of this state that her whole being was so present in the moment? A fully lived, meaningful life in a brief expression, like when a hand opens and reaches out to you and you know it's time, and you can feel that this moment is the most significant in your life. I still remember the gentleness of her last look and the reassuring smile, an undramatic knowing that there would be no more shoe repairs this time. Her entire hospital room was white, and she was the shining Light at its centre.

A few days later, my mum called me in from the backyard and told me that my sister had died during surgery. She was six years old.

She was a great, great master and I have often wondered if her name Lone had something to do with the English expression loner or lonely? The name comes from the old Danish name Abelone, which in turn comes from the Greek Apollonia. Apollonia was a Christian female martyr who was captured by a mob and tortured in Alexandria in AD 249. When threatened with death unless she repeated words her heart and conscience would not allow her to speak, she used a moment of release to jump on the stake herself.

My sister's death paralyzed me completely and turned everything upside down. Suddenly I remembered that day – a while before she was hospitalized – when the thought that she didn't have much time left had popped into my mind. It had been completely incomprehensible and horrible, and now it came back to haunt me like a nightmare. Was she dead because I had nourished that thought?

I started having painful movements in my body, something I experienced as two flower stems rising from my perineum and moving up my spine until they penetrated my skull and out into the cosmos. This went on every night for three years. Each morning, I would feel completely shattered, not only because it had been almost unbearably painful, but also because it was totally intimidating. There seemed to be no way out of the condition. Every night I would lie awake fighting not to fall asleep, as it was during the transition from wakefulness to sleep that the stems started to move. And once they started moving up my body, they were impossible to stop. The only way of reducing the pain was to try to give up all resistance and allow the expansion of the stems to continue. This is how I had my first out-of-body experiences. It wasn't until many years later when, as an adult, I started working with my teacher Calle Montségur that I got an explanation for the state I had found myself in. When the eros/libido is awakened in us, which usually happens in our early teens, the so-called kundalini force[6] also awakens in us. This awakening causes some – usually indefinable – movements in the perineum and up the centre of the spine, which are rarely painful and therefore almost never registered. However, if you experience a shock, as I did when my sister died, these kundalini movements can be released with such force that they can cause great pain.

---

[6] According to Tantric traditions in India and Tibet, kundalini is a primordial energy that flows from the lower part of the spine (root chakra) to the crown chakra. The energy can be activated spontaneously at certain periods in our lives like puberty, at traumatic events or through special yoga techniques in conjunction with spiritual work. When kundalini energy is awakened, for example through spiritual practices, it attempts to ascend, partially or completely, through a subtle channel *nadi* in the centre of the spine, called the *sushumna nadi*. Along the sushumna are seven chakras. The crown chakra is the main centre of all the chakras, in which the qualities of the other six become one once the kundalini has risen up through them all. When this has happened, the person is said to have attained spiritual enlightenment, *union mystica*, *nirvana* or *samadhi*, and is free from the wheel of karma. In the mystery schools of the Essenes and the Therapeutae, the chakras were called "The Seven Heavens".

At the same time, I began to develop the similarly agonizing ability of sensing other people's pain and thoughts, feeling their state of mind and seeing their often-hidden intentions and unconscious motives. I wasn't just being aware of other people's sensations and emotions, I was identifying and feeling what they were experiencing or suppressing. This was especially divisive because I suddenly realized that you can't always trust adults. The fact that they could say one thing, but at the same time think something else and then often do something completely different was incomprehensible and confusing. When I started to see the consequences of this mismatch and how it generally affected the lives of those involved, as well as the collective etheric field that we all share, it became an almost unbearable burden for me – a ten-year-old boy at the time, who already had enough to deal with.

At the age of eleven, I more or less stopped going to school. Instead, I disappeared deep into the forests north and south of my hometown, only showing up sporadically for an hour here and there. I guess my absence came in handy for the school too, as the teachers didn't seem to be able to handle the kind of grief and sadness I was carrying.

In the summer, I would sit leaning against a tree for hours watching butterflies and the smallest life on the forest floor. Time ceased to exist. The space around me suddenly became clear and distinct. I saw and understood how everything is connected. I began to see Light. The Light in the air. The Light around trees and plants. The Light that butterflies leave behind, which I later saw was part of the dust they shed, making them perfect bridges between physical and ethereal reality, right there where the world turned itself inside out. Even on grey days or when it was raining, I would wander aimlessly in the woods, surrounded by Light but separated from the world, indescribably lonely and full of sadness. In my schoolbag was my notebook with all my reflections.

One day, when winter had come, and it became too cold to go outside, I found shelter in the city cathedral. As I stepped into that church, I was greeted by the most beautiful organ music that cut through my pent-up grief and loneliness. The fact that I entered the church on the very day the organist was practising is not a coincidence but a divine gift. He was an extraordinary musician who lifted me up with his interpretations of Bach and Buxtehude and improvisations on well-known old hymns, which deeply moved me.

That day, I understood that it's one thing to be a good interpreter, but it's another to become one with the music you perform. That day, something happened to the burden I was carrying. That day, for the first time ever, I prayed to God. I asked to be given a sign that my sister was still alive somewhere, in Paradise or wherever God was supposed to be. My prayer must have hit the right frequency because I had barely finished praying when a small feather fell from the church vault and landed at my feet. Not only did I now know that God existed, but also that my sister was still alive – somewhere! There was no doubt in my mind. Now the question was, who or what was God and to what kind of place did my sister go?

For a long time after this experience, I visited the cathedral on the days when the organist practised, and also found out which days the organists of the other churches practised. In this way, I got a basic musical education in the churches of Aarhus. At home, I listened to the records my parents received once a month through the record club they were members of, as well as the discs by American artists who had hits in Europe. There were two records in particular that would inspire me and would have a lasting effect on me throughout my life. From the record club, it was Haydn's last symphony, No. 104 *London,* conducted by Eugen Jochum. From the lacquer discs, it was "How High the Moon" with Mary Ford and Les Paul that sent electricity through my 10-year-old body.

I was an early reader, and my first great experiences were with Mark Twain, Charles Dickens, Captain Marryat and

Kurt Held. But I experienced a completely new feeling of inner liberation when a family friend, David Jørgensen, gave me Jack London's *The Star Rover* shortly after my sister died. That book became my Bible as it assured me that there was more to life than meets the eye, and that there were other people who had experiences similar to mine. It tells the story of a life prisoner's experiences in San Quentin prison in California, where he was straitjacketed for days and weeks at a time, a punishment he had to endure again and again over several years. Under these inhuman conditions, he was able to leave his body and somehow travel into past incarnations. The novel is based on real events experienced by the life prisoner Ed Morrell, who was a friend of Jack London.

After I had read it, I was completely surprised that David had given me a book that covered out-of-body experiences and past lives. David was of Jewish descent and had been in a German concentration camp during World War II. He was a taxi driver and a gambler like my father, and I don't remember him ever talking about reincarnation or spiritual experiences. But I always had the feeling that he looked at me in a different way to anyone else in the stream of friends who visited my parents – that he was watching over me.

Not long ago, my cousin gave me a letter my mother wrote to my aunt a few months after my sister's death in 1960: "Thank you for the money for Lone's grave. It's all too much. We are doing well under the circumstances. We only have one big worry now, and that is that Lars is not the least bit interested in maths at school. He has opted out of extra lessons. When I express my concern, the boy replies: "Mum, don't worry about my future at all. I'll be fine!" He's so precocious and has his own opinions about everything. But even though he goes his own way, he is fortunately respected by both teachers and peers." The letter says neither anything about the boy's inner state nor about her own.

When I was 13, I was sent to Varde, to my "uncle" Hans and "aunt" Bertha.

In reality, we weren't related at all. Hans Sierich's parents had acted as foster parents for my grandfather Jens Peder Friedel Burkal, who had lost both his parents as a boy. I never forgot how he told me that he had to shoot blackbirds with bow and arrow to survive. It was a time of famine in Jutland, and many Danes emigrated to America and Argentina to seek their fortune there, which my grandfather did in 1909. In Argentina he met my grandmother, Petrea Nielsen, who also came from Jutland and had been sent across the Atlantic with her sister when her father had gambled away the farm they were living on. When she gave birth to my aunt Sylvia, they moved back to Denmark. Uncle Hans and my grandfather had been friends ever since.

I was supposed to spend the summer with Hans and Bertha, in the hope that the stay would release me from my introverted state. And it turned out to be true, but in a way very different from what my parents might have hoped for.

Hans and Bertha were incredibly caring. I never had the slightest doubt that they wanted the best for me. But the residential neighbourhood on the outskirts of Varde felt completely stagnant, and I still remember the slow and dreary sound of the old clock on the wall in the dining room, its hands almost moving backward, grinding second after second until time seemed to cease to exist.

I started fishing in the river, which was a 10-minute walk from Hans and Bertha's house, not because I was particularly into fishing, but because I needed to be alone. Fishing was an expected pastime for boys. I did not catch anything as I had no hook, only a cork on the line. After a few days alone by the river, a girl my age came walking on the other side. She called out to me if I was new to the area, and before I could answer, she took off her blouse and dress, got into the water wearing a blue swimsuit and swam over to me. We shared the packed lunch Bertha had given me and slowly I began to get a feel for the girl. She was doing all the talking, while I felt awkward and clumsy.

I must have fallen asleep, because suddenly I woke up and realized that she had disappeared. Had she been a dream or was she real? Then I remembered that the girl had pointed to a large stone, which she said was known as the "Sibyl's Stone" and that sometimes, in a cavity under the stone, you could find messages from another world. I was more or less disorientated as I made my way up to the stone and there, in the cavity the girl had pointed out, found a page torn out of a notebook on which someone had written "You fell asleep!"

The next day the girl in the blue swimsuit was waiting for me by the river. She was reading a story she had written in a notebook, which I realized had similar paper to the one on which the message from the previous day had been written. After a while, at her urging, I laid my head in her lap and let her voice lead me, mingling with the sound of the river's movement, in which the sun winked and embraced us in a moment I hoped would last forever. I had never felt so liberated and so happy. Gone were the shadows, the nightmares and the guilt.

Her story takes place in Germany just after the end of the First World War. A lonely soldier is returning from the battlefield across the shattered land to his hometown. But he feels so lost and devastated that he jumps off a bridge in despair, attempting to drown himself in the river. An old fisherman sees the soldier, pulls him out of the water and takes him to his home where he cares for him. When it's time for the soldier to move on, the old fisherman wants to make sure he gets there safely.

"If you're going to Munich, maybe I can help you. I have a good friend living there. I'll give you a letter for him. What is your name?"

The soldier hands him a soaked identity card as he continues to put on his dried clothes. When he's finished, the old fisherman hands him the letter. Then they say goodbye – and the girl pauses in her story.

"What did the letter say?" I ask.

The girl continues: "Dear Benjamin, would you do me the favour of giving this young man food and shelter until he finds work. His name is Adolf Hitler. Greetings from your friend Israel Cohen."

That night I couldn't get the thought out of my head how world history would have played out if the old fisherman had not intervened and saved the soldier. And where did the girl get that story from? Was it one she had made up herself or was it a description of a real event?

And so the weeks went by as I spent my days with the girl by the river. Every day we got closer and closer to each other. Often, we would just sit shoulder to shoulder and melt into each other and our surroundings. Other times I would read my writing, but I could listen to her read forever. One day, while fishing, I saw her as a dot in the distance travelling across the fields on the other side of the river toward me. She waved as she approached. Then she undressed, but this time she wasn't wearing the blue swimsuit underneath. Completely unabashed, wearing only the most beautiful Light, she got into the water and swam over to me. Averting my eyes as she stepped out of the water, I heard the sound of her feet in the narrow strip of sand that made up a tiny beach. Then I felt her hands on my face as she slid to her knees and kissed me fleetingly on the mouth. A force beyond anything I had ever experienced before lifted me up, up, up until I felt light as a feather.

The next thing I remember is us lying in the grass, embracing. As she stood up and walked down to the shore, she reminded me of a doe, a divine, luminous creature floating gracefully across the sunburned grass. Her free, uninhibited being dissolved my locked state. She waved to me from the other side, and I sat and followed her with my eyes until she was once again a tiny dot that became one with all the green.

For a whole week I went down and waited for her. But she didn't come. And the cavity under the Sibyl's Stone remained empty. This coincided with the last days of summer and it was time for me to go home too – back to Aarhus and everything that now seemed so far away. My whole being was torn apart.

That week, Hans, who was a trumpet player and member of the Musicians' Union, found an old Castello accordion in the basement. One afternoon, when I returned from the river, once again gutted and sad because the girl hadn't shown up, he put the accordion on the table in front of me and said that now it was mine. It was a marvellous instrument, slightly out of tune, but in such a way that it almost sounded like two accordions when you pulled the old bellows. I could sit for hours and conjure up one elongated, surreal landscape of sound after another, while I was completely filled with images of the girl replaying in my mind's eye, again and again. Occasionally Hans joined in with his trumpet, which must have sounded strange to everyone else, but for Hans and me it was bliss. Hans was not a man of many words. But with his trumpet he could talk. It was there that I got a sense of what it means to create music together with another human being. When you give yourself and dare to open up, even though you may be on unfamiliar ground, an ethereal field of affection and perhaps fervour is manifested, that makes unique and true communication possible. Technical ability is not essential or sufficient in itself. You must first and foremost possess an open heart. Then it's not possible to play "wrong".

Uncle Hans and Bertha followed me to the coach. It was there that I pulled myself together and asked if they knew 'the girl from the river', whom I described to them as best I could.

"About your age?" Bertha asked. She gave Hans a concerned look when I nodded. But before she could say anything else, it was Hans who set the record straight: "Well, that must surely be Sillesen's daughter, the one who drowned in the river last summer. They found her wearing a blue swimsuit. But how do you know about her?"

Yes, how? I was shaken but tried to pretend that I wasn't. The encounter with the girl and the fact that I might not see her ever again made my existential loneliness feel like an ice pick in my heart. Was this my destiny? Where was she? I found it hard to concentrate on anything but her.

It is clear in retrospect that what happened to me in Varde was due to the open and sensitive condition I was in after my sister's death. The girl, the note underneath the Sibyl's Stone, the story about Hitler, all played out on an etheric plane that had become accessible to me when I lay in the dreamy state of being half awake, half asleep at the riverbed where the girl had drowned. It was a mystical experience, intertwined with the impressions from the book *The Scourge of the Swastika* by Lord Edward Russell, that I had found on Hans and Bertha's bookshelf. We cannot know if the story about Hitler and the old Jew is true, but just imagine if ...

I stood in front of them, feeling helpless and overwhelmed but trying to keep my composure as best I could. Hans stuffed the book into my bag as I entered the bus that was taking me back to Aarhus.

Stories and images from the Nazi concentration camps were just more proof of the sickness of humankind and why the world looked the way it did. Why did it happen? Where did this indescribable hardening come from that can close its eyes and turn its back and just stand by while thousands of people are subjected to the most unspeakable and diabolically conceived torture. It was incomprehensible to me then, just as it is incomprehensible to me now, when it has become almost commonplace to dehumanize others to such an extent that we don't consider it anything out of the ordinary that some of our human family, groups or individuals, are subjected to suppression, exploitation, violence or murder. Is it something to do with the violence that now seems to be the main ingredient in the majority of films produced, just as the cynicism that surrounds it is boosted by a general sarcasm that may be necessary to deal with the violence, but which also perpetuates it? In any case, we seem to accept it in many of its costumes and forms, be it physical, mental or emotional violence – because not many people oppose it.

Violence makes us apathetic to such an extent that empathy has become a quality that can be talked about, but no longer really exists.

All over the world, even in the huts of the slums in the far East and in Africa, kids are playing war-games and watching violent movies. Violence is spreading like wildfire. Children have started to kill each other, children become soldiers, children are led to believe that it is OK to kick someone who is already lying down or to smash a bottle over someone's head or to shout at someone or to control or manipulate someone and to "assert your right". But what is "our right"? The right to what? Is there such a thing as justified violence?

3

A WORLD OUT OF SYNC

We never part from the heroes of our heart

The Danish philosopher Søren Kierkegaard's famous words, "Life must be understood backward, but it must be lived forward," would also prove to determine the development of my consciousness. Only long after my experiences I became conscious of their meaning.

I realize now that the first 15 years of my current life were part of a larger process of arriving here on Earth that I tried to avoid. While some parts of me didn't want to be here because I saw that physical reality was basically a step backwards from where I vaguely remembered I came from, I was paralyzed with the fear of leaving this very reality as I began to understand the whys and the hows of existence. And in the midst of this chaos, I found a belonging and peace in writing all my thoughts and observations on large yellow lined sheets of folio paper my grandfather had given me.

For a long time after I got home from Varde, I thought about the girl by the river. I found it hard to accept that she didn't belong to the physical world. I didn't understand it. I had been lying with my head in her lap, listening to her stories and watching her swim in the river – embracing her. And it didn't help that The Beatles had just released *She Loves You*. Was reality even real? All of my inner struggles and doubts were interspersed with nightly dreams in which my sister was running in the direction of a large lake with me close behind, and every time I was about to catch up with her, she disappeared into the lake and was gone.

I remember my relief when I woke up from these nightmares, and although during the day I was confronted with a reality that often scared me as well, I was getting used to this state of being both centered and beside myself, always sensing other people's suffering and pain – physical, mental and existential.

When I was faced with a person whom I could sense was not in balance because they spoke untruths or had hidden, unconscious or conscious, intentions, it had such an impact on my nervous system that I started shaking. Often, I had to close my eyes, turn away or simply excuse myself and leave the situation. Sometimes I would start humming to get out of or distract from the embarrassment I felt. Looking back, I understand that this reaction was more than just the hide-away attempt of a child who put their hands over their eyes, certain that no one could see them anymore. It was a way to change or transform the present frequency, which I unconsciously prevented from entering my field. It hurt me to experience a human being who felt the need to appear as something that was not in accordance with the truth. I understood that there were people who had convinced themselves that they were this shadow of themselves which they were projecting in different forms and expressions. They sometimes even contradicted themselves, depending on the other person standing in front of them.

Years later, when I had begun to study the Aramaic language[7] and read Chapter 12:25 in the *Gospel of Matthew* in Aramaic, I realized why I had reacted so strongly as a child to falsehoods and the imbalance they created.

---

[7] See Chapter 5 (The Kingdom of Heaven) and Chapter 19 (Aramaic Cornerstones) to read more about the Aramaic language.

"Every kingdom *(malkoot)* which you divide *(titpalagh)* against its *naphsha* will decay."

Or:

"Any kingdom that is divided from or does not honour its true destiny and purpose, cannot stand."

Kingdom in Aramaic, *malkoot,* means not just an earthly kingdom or a country, but a frequency, an area, a space, a sphere, an etheric energy field that envelops every living being, and is the essence of the reality I had seen as a child when we were playing cobbler. The reality that exists beyond the material or physical world we live in.

Titpalagh means to disconnect, divide or separate something, or to turn something upside down.

Naphsha is the true being, the very soul with its divine purpose and fate. Most people today experience themselves first and foremost as physical beings, who possess a range of feelings and an intellect. But the "kingdom" Yeshua speaks of in the *Gospel of Matthew* is a kingdom of Spirit, with which we are connected through the essence of our being. Consequently, that means that we humans are spiritual beings who in our physical existence are completely dependent on the etheric energy field mentioned. Without this etheric energy field, there would simply be no life on Earth.

When a person is unaware of the far-reaching consequences of lying and feels called to speak untruths or tries to appear as something other than what they truly are, it not only affects the individual's own energy field and integrity, but also that of those around them, where untruths infect and affect other people and, as in my case as a young child, sometimes even affect other people physically. When we more or less accept that it is perfectly normal for our politicians, for example, to say one thing and do another – i.e., have hidden agendas – it is easier to understand why our world looks the way it does.

The Yeshua quote testifies to a quantum physical, esoteric insight and understanding of human potential and the true perception of our reality. As mentioned in Chapter 1, in the *Gospel of Luke,* Yeshua speaks about this "kingdom" in the following way: "Remember, the Kingdom of Heaven *(Malkoota d'Shmeya)* is within you." This is an inner state in every human being and not a place. However, I ask you, dear reader, to reread these lines above about the "kingdom" being out of sync, just to remind yourself how significant they are and to really grasp what he is talking about. I may be the slow type myself, because I remember how I didn't really realize what Yeshua was introducing to us here until a relatively late stage in my life.

It was some days after my 13th birthday when my mother knocked on the bathroom door and tearfully stammered out that it had just been announced on the radio that US President John F Kennedy had been assassinated in Dallas. It happened on 22 November 1963. That evening, I wrote these words on a little piece of paper: "I, Lars Muhl, hereby declare that I will spend my life dedicated to freedom, enlightenment and justice." I hid the note in a cavity behind the wallpaper above my bed.

The next day, I gathered all the newspapers I could to read about the crime. I was certain that Lee Harvey Oswald, whom the police had caught and accused of the murder, was not the culprit. When he himself was shot dead two days later by a nightclub owner with Mafia connections, I knew that my hunch was right. Today, there is widespread debate with many voices strongly believing that Kennedy was the victim of a conspiracy to kill him and his brother, Robert Kennedy. When he too, as well as civil rights leader Martin Luther King, was assassinated, my former feelings of absolute trust in and adoration of America as the land of freedom and the future faded away. Especially Martin Luther King and his spiritual messages of unconditional love and non-violent resistance had left a burning and inspiring mark in my heart.

Looking back, I remember I felt like I was looking straight through a clear glass wall. Since the Second World War,[8] America has been promoted as the beacon of justice and prosperity that we in Europe have followed almost to the letter. Only a change of behaviour and the confrontation with the industrial and criminal economic forces that have been pulling the strings behind the scenes seducing and exploiting the Western world and the American people, can change the situation. America's corporations and governments have led their people into being the most belligerent nation of the last 70 years, leaving behind chaos and corruption wherever its successive governments have waged war under false pretences. It is also an example of how a line of rulers can undermine a nation when greed and lust for power prevail.

The Statue of Liberty was a French gift to America, her original name being "Liberty Enlightening the World". Standing on American soil, it implements America's role in establishing liberty in the world. I had been brought up to believe in the righteousness of that role, but now my trust felt betrayed, and the American dream seemed to become

---

[8] Different sources claim different numbers of so-called "casualties" in the Second World War: up to 85 million men, woman and children were killed in battles, in massacres, in mass-bombings, due to starvation or disease. (As a reference: In 2024, the current population of Denmark is 5.9 million people, Tokyo 37.1 million, California 39.1 million, the UK 69.2 million, Germany 84.4 million.) An unknown number of millions of people were wounded, crippled, have lost their homes through bombs, or through displacements, have lost their families, their belongings, their wealth. Some have lost literally everything they owned. Soldiers were held in prisons for years, so their families had no support from their husbands, fathers and sons. The men that came back were traumatized from the cruelty of their experiences. Some came back to cities of ruins, to missing, killed or similarly traumatized family members; others came back to broken relationships.

a nightmare. "Any kingdom that deviates from its true destiny cannot endure."

Of course, the same is true everywhere else in the world where rulers have disregarded the welfare of their citizens in favour of their own selfish interests, just as it is true for each of us.

Here is a quote from Robert F Kennedy, from a public speech he made in Indianapolis just hours after the assassination of Martin Luther King in April 1968:

"Let us dedicate ourselves to what the Greeks wrote so many years ago: To tame the savageness of man and make gentle the life of this world."

Was it because men like JFK, Marin Luther King and Robert Kennedy really wanted to make such words a reality that they were assassinated?

When I received a parcel in the post at the age of 14, my state of inner restlessness and loneliness changed. In 1964, not many children received letters or parcels unless they had a pen pal, which I did not. So, this was something very special. The parcel contained a book – *Gayan, Vadan, Nirtan* by Hazrat Inayat Khan, in a Danish translation. The fact that there was no return address on the parcel made the situation even more special, because who on earth wanted me to have this book and why did the sender not want me to know their identity?

That book saved my life. I opened it randomly and read: "If you will approach us, we will bow down and lift you up," and instantly I knew that I was no longer alone. There was someone around me, observing and being present.

In the book I could read that the author was a revered Sufi master and that this was a collection of his most famous aphorisms. The book not only talked about love, it *was* love, and reading it simply made me feel good. I was truly "lifted up". So, I read it over and over. That book was the start of a spiritual science study that has lasted ever since. In the colophon of the book, I found the address of the international headquarters of the Sufi Movement in Geneva, Switzerland, and sent off a letter requesting more information about the Master. Three weeks later, a leaflet about the Sufi Order and a purchase list of Khan's books arrived. I ticked off the title *The Mysticism of Sound* and enclosed a cheque for the Swiss francs the book cost. With the money I earned from selling milk and newspapers, I could buy the cheque at the bank with a power of attorney from my mother. After a month, the book arrived. It was through repeated readings of it that I slowly learned to understand English. A year later I ordered another book called *The Sufi Message of Hazrat Inayat Khan: Health, Mental Purification, the Mind World*. It was these books that formed my true schooling and became the foundation for everything I would do in the future.

It was also during these years that I spent time in trotting trainer Svend V. Pedersen's stable at the city's racetrack. As I said, my father was an inveterate gambler, so we often went to the track. I was more interested in the horses than the races and quickly realized that I had a natural connection to these amazing animals. Unfortunately, they weren't always treated equally well by the grooms, who didn't all consider animals to be sentient beings. To me, it clearly was the other way around: all horses are super sensitive, but there are people who seem devoid of any empathy.

Like most animals, horses can sense if you come with genuine intentions and a pure heart. It's inherent in them to be able to sense the "realm", or etheric energy field that we humans radiate and bring with us everywhere. Therefore, it's especially important to understand and remember this when we approach a horse or other animals. We should just try to be at peace with ourselves. If we are simply honest and open about our condition, we can be both grief-stricken and unbalanced – the horse can then prove to be the best healer we can meet. Standing still and letting the horse approach you and standing forehead to forehead or cheek to cheek with it is one of the most powerful experiences there is. Horses or other animals subjected to force and training can be damaged for life. Many of the methods used to "correct" horses usually have the complete opposite effect. You may be able to break the horse's will, but at the same time you turn it into a shadow of its former self. For example, if a horse doesn't have an innate desire for or take pleasure in trotting, it's a crime to force it to do so. This is the case with all living beings, including humans. On the other hand, I have also seen horses that clearly loved to trot and were very keen to compete. The most valuable lesson I learned from working with horses was that one needs to be present and have complete trust in God Consciousness to truly know another being, horse or human.

4

WHAT WE GIVE IS WHAT WE GET

The sun will ease the rain of pain

I was 14 years old when it became clear to me how we humans, each one of us, are responsible for our own reality. We create it through everything we think, feel, say and do, whether we know it or not. Everywhere we go, we leave a trace, not only in the physical world, but especially in the ethereal space around us. This was not only the effect caused by people who were not true to themselves or to others as I experienced over and over, it was also a reality in my own life. When I nurtured negative thoughts or became depressed, it affected my life instantly, creating sadness and separation. When I prayed, things would change and open my heart, and I would start to see other people and my circumstances in a brighter light.

I began to realize that the definition of God is dependent on our perception. I could feel the presence of a force in my own body and in the energetic fields around other people, animals or plants. I could identify this force as the cause of every breath and heartbeat. By then I was sure that nothing in our world is random.

Every so often, I would experience glimpses of another reality hidden behind the physical when the veil would suddenly disappear, and I would stare into a luminous universe of crystals interactively connected to each other via the finest vibrating beams of Light. The flashes lasted only a moment but opened up a certainty within me that I now needed to learn to live with – and trust. Many years later, I read in Marcus Aurelius' *Meditations*, which date from around AD 160:

"Always see the universe as one living Being with one substance and one Soul. Be aware that everything created is connected with the cosmic Consciousness of this Being. Be aware also that everything moves under the influence of this Being, co-operating in the creation of all events by constantly spinning fine threads in this incredibly complicated web."

Was it these thoughts that the father of quantum physics, Max Planck, consciously or unconsciously, picked up in 1944, when he wrote the following:

"All matter originates and exists only by virtue of a force … We must assume behind this force the existence of a conscious and intelligent Mind. This Mind is the matrix of all matter."

It was not possible for me to talk to anyone about these visions and realizations. The few times I tried, I was met with no resonating or at least interested responses, only disapproval, mockery or incomprehension. Even today, people who have had unusual experiences are still ridiculed. The whole issue of UFOs and the people who have reported having seen them, and even having been in contact with beings from outer space, has for years caused them to be considered fantasists or deranged people who just wanted to attract attention. Time and time again, these experiences have been refuted on the grounds that life elsewhere in the universe or space travel of this nature cannot take place. After all, how would it be possible to defy gravity or travel light years when *we* are incapable of doing so? If only we knew better. Because that's exactly what we as humans are capable of.

Unfortunately, it's often ignorance and resistance to everything we don't understand or don't want to understand that sets the agenda. The fact that something is unusual or unfamiliar doesn't necessarily mean that it doesn't exist or isn't real or true. It's very good to be discerning, but the reason for any analysis, assessment or judgement should be based on openness and experience, not bias and fear. We are all victims of this ignorance, and countless are those who over the years have presented new visions or shared extraordinary experiences and lost either their reputations, their livelihood or their lives in the process.

It is rarely easy to be a first mover. Take Yeshua, who incarnated to set an example for humanity, teaching us the reality of unconditional and uncompromising love by his very being. Yeshua, around whom a church and a religion, Christianity, has been created. He in whose name we are baptized and confirmed. But who was he and what is his role today? Who are we?

Just think of all the topics and contents that are gullibly believed to be important for children to learn in school, and which are therefore pounded into our heads, turning us into some kind of well-meaning but fundamentally ignorant robots. At no point do we learn what should be the most important thing: what is a human being?

So very much would change in our world and our lives, if we would teach and share knowledge of our being and our gifts in our pedagogic and academic curriculums and start to see education as a means to find and foster the talents and interests of each and every one of our children.

It was in Hazrat Inayat Khan's books that I found words for the certainty I had experienced ever since I began to be able to see beyond external reality as a child. This meant that my introverted state changed, and I stepped into the world. However, my loneliness still lingered. Although it felt as if

I was settling into it, at times with comfort and at other times in despair, I knew I needed to find a way to be in the world. The one thing I was sure of was that I had to write. Through my job at the racecourse, I learned that a local newspaper, *Aarhus Amtstidende*, needed a journalist with an understanding of equestrian sports. The newspaper was known among punters at the track for its eminent stable tips, but now the journalist who passed them on had died.

Amtstidende was a right-wing newspaper with an address on the high street. When I entered the small newsroom, I realized that there was only one employee sitting there. It turned out to be the person in charge, chief editor Due. After a quick interview, I was sent down the street to cover the opening of a new fashion store, Boutique 22. In the shop window, a band called Shaking Phantoms with singer Poul Erik Veigaard on drums was playing. I wrote a small review and returned to editor Due, who crossed out most of my notes, added a headline and the article was ready for print. It took Due five minutes to hammer out a "press card" on a piece of typewriter paper and I was hired. What I didn't know at that time was that the newspaper was heading for bankruptcy and that the only employees besides me were a bookkeeper and a cleaning lady. But what I also didn't know was that there would come a day when I would meet the singer from Shaking Phantoms again.

It happened two years later when I joined the beat group Daisy.[9] I had always been musical but had never had any ambitions to become a musician. But I was so lonely and introverted that I realized I couldn't possibly function in the world alone. No human being has come here to be and work for themselves. It was this loneliness and my innate musicality that, among other things, led me into the destiny of Daisy's

---

[9]   In my book *Vi kom svævende – Historien om et band (We Came Floating – The Story of a Band)*, Sacred Seed Publishing, you can read more about Daisy.

community. Daisy was a local beat group that emerged in late 1967. I joined on the recommendation of the group's guitarist Frank Lorentzen, and it was clear to me from the start that I had come home when I first entered Poul Erik Veigaard's room in Aabyhøj, a suburb of Aarhus, where the band was based. It wasn't just five lads united around the same musical dedication, but five souls who had found each other in this incarnation again because they had something in common and something they had to experience together as a group.

Poul Erik was the lead singer and Daisy was his vision. It was the first time in my 16 years of life that I was genuinely received and welcomed for who I really was, without having to hide the parts of me that others couldn't seem to recognize or accept. There were no restrictions, but an openness from everyone to the world of spirit that I had not encountered before. This resulted in many long conversations of a philosophical nature on esoteric and metaphysical topics, but also immersion in a very special album, *Friends* by the Beach Boys, which had a great impact on me for many years to come. For months we rehearsed the choral arrangements of the songs on this magical album, which to this day continues to have a healing effect on me. It was, and still is, an album that not many people know about. *Friends* was the follow-up to the Beach Boys' *Smiley Smile* and was a far cry from the surf that had characterized the band.

Daisy debuted with a bang on New Year's Eve 1968, resulting in a flurry of concert activity and the band quickly gaining a large fan base. It was before the days of festivals, which meant there weren't many opportunities for a band like Daisy to play in Denmark in the summer. So, a two-month tour to Israel was organized. It was a journey that had a transformative effect on everyone in the band and was part of the reason we had come together.

For me, travelling to Israel was an encounter with the land where the life and work of Yeshua had taken place. And again, just as with joining Daisy, I had the feeling of coming home. Imagine being 17, coming to a place that has had a magnetic pull for my whole being, travelling with a group of boys who I also felt were my family and making music together: I was in a state of total happiness. The band consisted of Frank, Poul Erik, Flemming Walsøe, Egil Madsen and myself. With us was Robert Hauschildt, who had given up his position as lead singer in the band The Old Man and The Sea to join Daisy on this journey. We had come to know Robert through the numerous gigs that Daisy had shared with The Old Man and The Sea. Poul Erik and Robert had bonded, and later when I came to know Robert's spiritual and philosophic interests along with his passion for classical and world music, I understood why he wanted to join us on this once-in-a-lifetime experience. For many years to come he became like an older brother to me.

We drove down through Germany, over the Austrian and Swiss Alps, through a bruised Yugoslavia with its political unrest, earthquakes and corruption which had left the country in grave poverty.

We continued into Greece to catch the ferry from Piraeus to Haifa in Israel. We travelled in Robert's band van, which was so worn out it was amazing that it could carry six people with all our equipment and gear so far without any major mishaps. Once we arrived in Israel and were settled in Hotel Kedem in Tel Aviv, a hectic touring life began, playing every day of the week except the Sabbath. Once a fortnight, we also had a day off where we had the opportunity to see some of Israel's countless tourist attractions.

It was on such a day that I had an experience which had a decisive impact on the direction my life would take from that moment on. We were driven to the Dead Sea to see the ruins at Qumran, which were believed to have been a monastery for a spiritual community called the Essenes, who are thought to be the authors of the Dead Sea Scrolls found in nearby caves in 1947. During the 1950s, these ruins had been excavated and we were now about to visit them. The team included a small group of archaeologists for whom this was a study trip. It was during the tour that the guide explained what the different rooms had been used for.

As we had approached the site of Qumran, I began to have a strange feeling as if I had been there before. Now I suddenly heard myself interrupting our guide after he had just informed us that the room in which we were standing was once the Essene dining hall. "I'm sorry, but the dining room was in that room over there," I chipped in, pointing to the room next door. It all happened so fast that I didn't have time to think. I saw how my remark not only embarrassed the guide, also my friends looked at me with incomprehension. But only until one of the archaeologists, a German professor, leaned forward behind me and said to the guide: "I think the young man is right!"

Not a sound could be heard after these words. Now that his expertise was in question, the guide brought the tour to an early finish, so our group was left to our own devices. For me, my reaction was as surprising as it had been for the others.

The odds of being on the tour with this German professor and experiencing the same awareness about the structures of the ruins felt like a cosmic arrangement and confirmation, as well as a big inner push. From that moment on I had only one thing on my mind: finding out who these Essenes had been.

Another piece of information that came to me in the car on the way back to Tel Aviv was that the ruins at Qumran were not the remains of a monastery, but of a university. This also made much more sense since the guide had said at the beginning of his tour that it was not yet understood how 2,000 Essenes could have lived in these buildings. They didn't. They lived along the shore of the Dead Sea. Ein Gedi, on the plateau, where the large kibbutz now stands, was a settlement in which the majority of the Essenes lived. The university at Qumran was looked after and served by about 20 members of the sect. It felt like another inner certainty I just knew to be true.

But the Israel tour did not go smoothly. One day, the doors to our two rooms at Hotel Kedem were ripped open and a team of police stormed in. We were ordered to stand with our faces to the wall while they searched everything. After they found a few lumps of hashish, we were taken to Israel's toughest prison, Abu Kabir, on the outskirts of Tel Aviv. There we spent a week in the most primitive conditions – stone barracks without blankets, cold water without soap or towels and a hole in the centre of the cell that was the only place to carry out one's necessities. After a week, we were brought before a judge and released on bail.

Encountering the reality of prison and the criminals who languished there changed us from boys to young men in the time of these seven days. The violence in the prison alone was shocking. On our daily walk in the yard, we saw how murderers and rapists were kept in holes about 3 metres by 3 metres with iron bars over them. During the day a roasting oven and at night an icebox. Every time the other prisoners passed these holes, they spat on the poor wretches, who responded by throwing themselves around like wild animals and shouting curses. And all this happened while a man set foot on the moon for the first time according to our historical records, with the words: "One small step for man, one giant leap for mankind." Standing in a prison yard in Israel, chained to a fellow prisoner, this solemn proclamation for mankind seemed completely meaningless to me.

The day we were due to leave Israel and travel back to Denmark, I sat outside a café in Tel Aviv early in the morning with a cup of coffee and watched the city come to life. On the pavement on the opposite side, some teachers were walking with a group of kindergarten children. I don't know if it was the sight of them that caused me to be suddenly thrown out of my body and lifted about 20 metres into the air at high speed, from where I watched the whole scene. In an instant I realized that the Israel trip would be the end of the band that had brought us on this journey. For a moment, I wondered if I should stay behind in the country I had come to love so much and where I felt I belonged. With a spinning head and pent-up shoulders, I found myself back on my seat outside the café.

I was far from ready to leave. It would also be a goodbye to Shimon, a boy of about 13 who went to school opposite the apartment on Hayarkon Street 297 where we were living. One day, while I was sitting on the porch, he stopped and said hello to me. I asked if he would like to come in and join me for a cup of tea. He did. There had been all kinds of rumours about Daisy, and the prison stay was all over the news, so we had become sort of reverse celebrities and the subject of much interest. But I soon realized that it wasn't Daisy's new status that had made him stop at our porch. He recognized me on a different level. This meeting was the start of a short but meaningful friendship. Shimon's father had died during the Six Day War two years earlier. He now lived with his mother and two sisters. I felt an indescribable unity with him. It was as if we came from the same place. In him, I recognized the same paths I had travelled when I was his age.

One day he gave me a piece of silver jewellery with the most beautiful filigree that he had made himself in his uncle's silversmith workshop where he worked. He told me that the jewellery depicted eternal life through eternal birth and eternal death. Inside a silver filigree ball, he had placed a piece of King Solomon's cedar tree. On top of the sphere was a double cone, the tips of which pointed out outward into eternity and inward, home to God.

When I came back from the café, he was waiting for me to say goodbye. I gave him a silver chain with my finger ring decorated with a phoenix, which he had often admired. He broke down crying and begged me to stay, hugging me as if he would never let go. I mumbled a few words, trying to find a way to soothe him and hide my feelings of helplessness, because inside I was crying too.

Then, he let go, jumped over the edge of the porch and disappeared running down Hayarkon Street. That was the last time I saw him.

Maybe we all feel lonely, and maybe all our desperate attempts to be loved are the opposite of what we came here for. With a tight chest and a heavy heart, I packed the rest of my few belongings. There had to be a way to break this wall of helplessness. "What we give is what we get!" I wrote in my diary on our way back to Denmark.

5

IN SEARCH OF TRUTH

Those who are dear are always near

Back home, I immediately started to study the Essenes and the Dead Sea Scrolls. I came to understand very quickly that it wouldn't be quite as straightforward as I had assumed. Finding Danish books on the theme in 1969 was a challenge. The most interesting research was in English. In times before we had immediate access to everything on the internet, my only option was the State Library, which fortunately was in Aarhus. There I borrowed various translations of the Dead Sea Scrolls, along with a collection of books on the Essenes that were available at the time; the majority of them had to be obtained from abroad. The books I remember the most were Arthur Lillie's *Buddhism in Christendom – Jesus the Essene* from 1887; Edouard Schuré's *The Great Initiates* from 1889 and a book by Jeffrey Furst, *Edgar Cayce's Story of Jesus*, which had just been published the year before in 1968. Not only did the book tell a previously unknown story of Yeshua and his affiliation with the Essenes, but it was also the story of America's most famous seer of recent times, Edgar Cayce, aka "the sleeping prophet". That book was another gift from the beyond that helped me understand my own experiences.

However, Cayce's interpretation of the Essenes was very difficult to reconcile with the writings that these people supposedly left behind. While the Dead Sea Scrolls mostly indicated that the writers were part of a rigid patriarchal hierarchy that adhered to the strictest rules, Cayce's visions were different and somehow disburdening and liberating to read. Much of the information about the Essenes that came to the sleeping Cayce was a paradox to him, as it was totally foreign to the waking Cayce and his way of thinking and in stark contrast to his fundamentalist Christian upbringing. Throughout his life, Cayce read the Bible at least once a year from beginning to end, and he never deviated in his channelings from the familiar stories when talking about his beloved Yeshua. Yet these stories were now expanded with many details that put Yeshua's life trajectory and the entire Bible into a new perspective. Cayce shared a wealth of information about the Essenes: to his own surprise, he learned from one of his readings one day that they were the brotherhood in which Yeshua had been raised and educated.

Before a so-called "psychic reading", Edgar Cayce loosened his laces, tie, belt and shirt cuffs to free up the circulation in his body. Then he lay down on his sofa. If the reading was about physical problems, he lay down with his head facing south and his feet facing north. If it was a "life reading" about the client's current or past life, he lay down in the opposite direction. He then placed both hands on his forehead, stimulating a place on our body and in our energetic field that triggers the inner sight called the "third eye", and said a prayer. He then waited a few minutes until he saw a flash of brilliant white Light, sometimes with a golden colour. This was the signal that there was contact. When the Light did not appear, he knew that it was not possible to give a reading to the person present.

After the Light phenomenon had disappeared, he placed his hands over the solar plexus while his breathing now became deep and rhythmic from the diaphragm. During these preparations, he usually lay with his eyes open, without registering the physical reality that surrounded him. When his eyes began to blink, his wife or secretary assisting him knew it was possible to ask him questions on behalf of the client. The only one who wasn't aware of the whole procedure or any of the content that his voice would be sharing was Edgar Cayce himself. Therefore, it came as a shock to him when he read some of the stenographed answers he, or whoever it was, had given about Yeshua and the Essenes. Cayce himself said that the information came from the so-called Akashic records.

There were several questions I was grappling with in the early 1970s, because something didn't make sense. The image that Cayce conjured up of these Essenes did not fit with the writings they were claimed to have authored. After some time of speculation, a new mind-image emerged. Could it be a misunderstanding of the language the scriptures were written in, a wrong way of interpreting the Hebrew and Aramaic letters? Again, it was only an inner certainty that had appeared and drove me to question the established translations and interpretations, as I had no intellectual or linguistic insight into the language of the scrolls at that time.

But I felt I was on the right track – I just did not know where to look for more knowledge. Instead, in the years that followed, while Frank, Eigil and I were trying to keep Daisy together without our lead singer, my understanding of God[10] opened up through a series of nightly dreams. These were possibly ignited by my reading of the *Book of Enoch*, which I was studying at the time. As Enoch, in my dreams I felt I was transported to a higher dimension where God Consciousness was present in its most clarified way, nourishing the different souls that were being prepared for incarnation. I was the silent witness. I knew that the clarity I experienced was the Consciousness we call God, and when I woke up from these dreams I had over a period of two weeks, I felt this clarity filling my whole being. When I walked down the streets, I really understood that there is nothing that is not due to Divine Consciousness or included in it. It is omnipresent. Everything originates from it and everything is interactively connected through it.

[10] See my book *The God Formula*.

God Consciousness is eternal and unchanging. It embraces all forms of mutability without changing itself. All apparent contradictions and dualities are contained and transformed in God Consciousness where they become One in the One. Everywhere we go, God is. Yet it is possible to exist without being in conscious contact with God.

The physical world is impermanent and limited while the non-physical realms are infinite and eternal. I call the reality of the infinite and eternal realms "the World of Answers", to which we humans have access at all times while we are incarnated here in the physical world – "the World of Questions".

Everything in the physical world is changing. Change, as in movement, transformation, expansion, unfolding seems to be the basic premise of life itself. And it is when we humans resist change that suffering arises.

In *Genesis* we read that God created man in His[11] image. What is this image? What does God look like? Image in this context means *likeness*. In his outstanding five-volume work from 1963, *Philosophy of the Masters*, Huzur Maharaj Sawan Singh puts it this way:

"God is the great storehouse of Consciousness. God is the manifestation of clarity and a treasure house of intelligence. God is the repository of love and compassion. God is the whole, and each of us is a part of Him. He is the whole. The essence of which our souls are made emanates from the source of all souls, God. If we are a drop of Consciousness, then He is the ocean of Consciousness. He is the sun of the essence of Consciousness, and we are its rays. Every particle is

[11] In Aramaic "God" is perceived as the Heavenly Parent that is both masculine and feminine. Wherever I read the masculine form (Heavenly Father God), I replace it with the understanding of a unified Being (Heavenly Mother Father God/The Heavenly Source of All Being).

a part of the whole. Our real substance is a part of that whole which is called God."

So, we carry this God Consciousness within us. And we live in it, just as everyone around us does. "The sun shines on everyone", the saying goes. But at the same time, we were also given free will so that through the attitudes we embody, the beliefs we follow, the choices we make and the actions we take, we are co-creators of what we perceive to be reality. We can kill, develop murderous weapons, deceive, steal and lie and thus turn our backs on the qualities and frequencies of the all-harmonious God Consciousness. We can do whatever we want. But everything we do has consequences. Not only for ourselves, but also for the world around us.

The first atomic bombing on Earth, for example, triggered immediate action from other inhabitants of the Milky Way and the rest of the universe. This was the start of a storm of enquiries to the world's governments from people who believed they had observed what were dubbed "flying saucers" in the 1940s, but which we know today as UFOs (Unidentified Flying Objects). Some witnesses reported direct contact with alien beings from outer space, while others gave accounts of being abducted by extraterrestrial beings and subjected to various clinical tests before being released again.

As mentioned before, for many years, attempts were made to ridicule such witnesses and then explain away all these reports, while today many of the classified government documents that have been hidden from the public are being released. Since then, hundreds of astrophysicists, astronauts, pilots, military personnel, intelligence officers[12] and even former president Jimmy Carter have come forward to recount their experiences, many of which include accounts of contact

---

[12] See Dr Steven Greer's *Disclosure-Project* and Dr John E Mack's books *Passport to the Cosmos* and *Abduction*. See also the documentary *Bob Lazar: Area 51 and Flying Saucers*.

with so-called alien beings from other civilizations in space since the 1940s.

Military intelligence agents report that beings from other star systems in telepathic conversations have justified their presence here on the grounds that the detonation of a weapon as powerful as the atomic bomb by earthlings also affects the rest of the universe. These beings have warned the people of Earth not to continue their destructive development, but also let us know that the creative force we call God is not only responsible for the creation of Earth and the universe humans inhabit but has created all universes and all beings there. The aliens tell us that this force must not be used with any harmful intentions and its creation must not be manipulated. If we ignore it – instead of acknowledging its power, which is our very essence, and start co-creating with this essence – those who do not recognize these aspects of life will end up destroying their livelihoods and their human selves.

Today's challenge is that we are bombarded with news of the most horrific acts committed by humans against other humans and animals, to such an extent that it somehow hardens us. We choose to become more and more passive. And perhaps this is a natural reaction, because we feel powerless and don't know what to do. The most terrible atrocities take place every single day, every hour, every minute, somewhere on the planet. Take the atomic bombings of Hiroshima and Nagasaki on 6 and 9 August 1945. What actually happened?

Few people know about Claude Eatherly. He was the commander of the reconnaissance plane that first flew over Hiroshima. It's a beautiful day. The sun is high and bright in the sky, not a cloud in sight. He's the one who reports the weather conditions to the plane with the bomb that is following him about one hour behind. They drop 20 kilotons of TNT on the heads of 200,000 unsuspecting Japanese people, who are either killed on the spot or die a slow and painful death over the following weeks. The city is literally levelled to the ground. When he had given the all-clear for the drop of the bomb, Claude Eatherly did not realize the scale of what was about to happen. Only three of the pilots involved in this "mission", as well as the men behind the bomb and a select few generals, are aware of the scale of the apocalypse. They have witnessed the first tests in New Mexico, now they get to see the effects of the monster on real, living people. Those who drop the bombs will be just as shocked as those who receive them. Despite the madness of this act, it is also considered by some as perfectly normal, and promoted as a necessity to prevent a greater loss of lives in the ongoing war.

Will we ever learn to solve conflicts without violence? Will those who decide to drag the human family into violent acts or omissions ever feel the brutality and pain outside of the control rooms?

A telegram, sent by a delegate of the International Committee of the Red Cross, Fritz Bilfinger, on 30 August 1945 from Hiroshima to the ICRC office in Tokyo, speaks for itself:

"Visited Hiroshima thirtieth conditions appalling stop city wiped out eighty percent all hospitals destroyed or seriously damaged inspected two emergency hospitals conditions beyond description fullstop effect of bomb mysteriously serious stop many victims apparently recovering suddenly suffer fatal relapse due to decomposition of white blood cells and other internal injuries now dying in great numbers stop estimated still over onehundredthousand wounded in emergency hospitals located surroundings sadly lacking bandaging materials medicines stop"

A century has been divided into two realities, before 1945 and after 1945. The great expectations of the invention are more than fulfilled. One war is over, another can begin.

The bombs over Hiroshima and Nagasaki detonated in the air. A fireball is formed with temperatures comparable to the temperature inside the sun. In a matter of seconds, the fireball grows to a size of over a kilometre in diameter. A part of the energy released spreads out from the fireball as pressure waves. All buildings without special armouring are levelled to the ground. The shockwave is followed by a storm with a speed of approximately 80 metres per second (180 miles per hour). A hurricane is moving 33 metres per second (75 miles per hour). Another part of the fireball's energy is emitted as heat rays, partly as visible light and partly as infrared rays. The intense radiation causes burns to people and anything flammable in a radius of 15 kilometres (9 miles) from the centre of the explosion. Eyes are melting in the eye sockets of those looking into the fireball. The skin is ripped off everyone. Men, women, children and animals are burned, crushed, knocked over, punctured, irradiated, drowned. The rest of the energy is released as radioactive radiation. It does no material damage but has an incalculable impact on all living things. The radioactive dust left by the bombings is whirled up into the atmosphere and can float and fall wherever the wind blows. The effects last for decades and will impact the coming generations with birth defects and deformed children, radioactive fallout, dead trees, plants and infertile soil.

After the "successful mission" those who carried it out were hailed as heroes. Claude Eatherly and his crew were honoured and decorated with awards. But Eatherly didn't want to be recognized as a hero. Not after what he had experienced. He felt a moral responsibility for his action, his nights were filled with nightmares and his conscience led him to writing letters of apology, sending cheques to Hiroshima and getting in contact with pacifist groups. He called for "a re-examination of our willingness to surrender responsibility for our thoughts and actions to some social institution such as the political party, trade union, church or State." At the same time, his life took many obscure turns, he was arrested on different occasions for petty thefts and hospitalized in a psychiatric hospital, where he was diagnosed with a guilt complex. However, there was no complex from Eartherly's point of view. In his eyes, he was guilty. There are different accounts of the rest of his life, one being that he was separated from his wife and children and permanently hospitalized and declared insane.

Now the question is: were Hiroshima and Nagasaki a crime against humanity like Hitler's concentration camps? During the Nuremberg Trials, some of the accused defended themselves by claiming that they had simply obeyed orders and were therefore innocent. However, the Allied tribunal ruled that anyone who acts, regardless of orders, is responsible for their actions. Claude Eatherly insisted on his guilt and responsibility. In doing so, he condemned not only himself, but the government, the general staff, perhaps even an entire nation, which is unheard of. That's why Eatherly had to be locked up. He later died of cancer in a hospital.

As said before, everything in our universe, and all other universes, is subject to the Law of Light. It is implicit in God Consciousness, with which it is one. The Law acts as a mirror in which humans and all other beings can reflect themselves at all times. If the reflection is not in accordance with the Law, we have the opportunity to change our behaviour until it is once again in sync with the Law. When we break the Law of Light, it affects us in different ways. It is not a punishment, just neutral appearances – consequences of our own making, which appear in a way that allows us to recognize, understand and make amends for our actions that were not based on kindness.

The Indian Vedas describe this "cause and effect" process as *karma* (action; the path of consequences). When we understand why we are haunted by the same kind of bad luck over and over again, we eventually realize that we can put an end to our misfortune by actively and intentionally changing our attitudes and our behaviour. It is through experiential understanding that we begin to walk a more purposeful and conscious path. This is what the Indian Vedas call *dharma* (responsibility; the path of duty). Any insight gained through experience obliges us to take responsibility for it, and to integrate its teachings so we can always be the best version of ourselves as possible.

Divine insights and experiences happen if we follow our conscience and honour the Law of Light.

Most people have lived through countless incarnations. We have been both executioner and victim, king and slave, rich and poor, man and woman. The question is how many times we have to experience all these roles before we realize and truly understand who we are and what we are doing here. Every human being is in itself the essence of all the experiences it has had in all the past incarnations it has lived through, as well as the essence of all experiences it will have in any of its future incarnations.

One evening after a meditation I received the following vision: God Consciousness creates in the way of projection, where a part of the non-physical world is turned inside out and an image of the non-physical is created, which is then manifested physically. Just like when you take a picture with an analogue camera. Afterwards the film is being developed into a set of negatives. These negatives are being further developed into positives, and their images now make sense to the naked eye. And just as an old photograph eventually yellows and disappears, so too does the physical (if it is not consciously kept in an activated state), while the power that resided in it and the intentions behind it return to their starting point, God the Great Consciousness.

Maybe you have heard of the Shroud of Turin. It is a cloth with an image of a crucified man, stung by a spear in his side, with marks from being whipped by a Roman scourge, and with marks around the head from a crown of thorns. The cloth is proved to be from the time of Yeshua and made in Jerusalem. It wasn't before it was photographed in the late 1890s that the researchers found out that the image on the cloth is a negative. It became positive and visible with all its details – on the negative of the film! In other words, a reverse creational process from the physical to the non-physical had somehow happened here.

It is believed by the scientists who worked with the shroud that the man on the image is Yeshua in the very moment his soul left his body, and that it was a "burst of conscious Light"[13] emanating from him that created the image. The Shroud of Turin has been called the world's first photograph.

Yet, the authenticity of the shroud was challenged by a radiocarbon dating done in 1988, showing that the real date of the cloth was somewhere between 1260 and 1390. It wasn't until scientific work done on the shroud in the 1990s discovered that the cloth used in the radiocarbon dating process stemmed from a part of the shroud that had been exposed to a fire during the Middle Ages. All later tests unequivocally indicate that the shroud is two thousand years old and specifically comes from Jerusalem. It is the only one-dimensional image from before the computer age, that carries three-dimensional properties from which it can be turned into a hologram. Scientist Peter Schumacher, who invented the VP-8 image analyzer, regards this as unique and compelling evidence of the cloth's authenticity.

People who are aware and connected to God Consciousness differ from people who have no understanding or experience of it in their approach to life; they have different goals and desires. A God Conscious person does nothing that does not contribute to developing God Consciousness. Therefore, the world needs God Conscious people to pave the way for other people. Words are poor in this respect, as it is only through the power of example that true communication of God Consciousness can take place.

[13] See *A Burst of Conscious Light* by Dr Andrew Silverman; *The Turin Shroud* by Ian Wilson and Barrie Schwortz; and *The Shroud of Turin: First Century after Christ!* by Giulio Fanti and Pierandrea Malfi.

It is a mystery to me that we can celebrate great scientists such as Max Planck, Albert Einstein, Niels Bohr and David Bohm while completely neglecting the universal religiosity or God Consciousness that runs like a common thread through their work. Many books have been written about these scientists by people who seem to be so scared of spirituality that they have found it necessary to close their eyes to this important aspect of these mystics' work. What made Einstein keep a copy of the *Bhagavad Gita* and of Madame Helena Blavatsky's epochal work *The Secret Doctrine* in his laboratory? There is hardly a female spiritual scientist who has been subjected to more slander and ridicule than Blavatsky. And why is that? Because many physicists and science enthusiasts had no idea what she was talking about and apparently did not have the interest to research her work or the intuitive understanding to recognize her contribution to the realization of what a human being is and in what reality we exist. Accepting her thoughts and experiences meant that many of the comfortable conclusions that had been reached and from which new theories had been developed would have to be revised. I believe that the reason Einstein kept these two books in his laboratory and – as witnessed by his family and friends – often opened them randomly, was because he found thoughts in them that inspired his own work as a physicist.

The 1940s rise of quantum physics seriously challenged theology. Quantum physicists like Max Planck, Albert Einstein and David Bohm introduced a whole new way of viewing God, creation and humanity's relation to the universe and the concept of eternity. For years theological treatises tried to explain many of the seemingly inexplicable details in the Bible but without clarifying them. And very many treatises were based on previous, erroneous theologies, so that to this day it is still not understood what the hero of Christianity, Yeshua the Nazarene, was trying to pass on to us and what reasons he presented to us – not only in words, but as experiences with himself as an example.

But the devil is in the detail, as the saying goes – while God is always in the whole! Therefore, all details must be seen from the standpoint of the whole and brought back into the awareness of belonging to the whole. The detached and isolated dots must be connected. No harmonious solutions can ever be found without this awareness.

At a point in my search for more insight into the scriptures, I had to face the fact that my lack of academic education and method was a stumbling block that forced me to trust my intuition and visions even more. And it was through intuition I began to nourish the thought that there had to exist a hidden language that we in our time had forgotten – an etheric language that was once known in the distant past. So, from the mid-1970s, I began an intense search in all the world's great religious traditions, reading everything through the eye of intuition, while at the same time I had an inexplicable feeling that this mysterious language was actually to be found in the very God Consciousness with which all humans have been endowed.

But it was also a time when I was confronted with being in the world. Finding a place. I started writing lyrics and music that expressed the loneliness that kept being my closest companion, despite all the spiritual insights I gained and the friends I found in the band. Daisy's only album, *The Lonesome Brigade*, which blues musician Peter Thorup produced, was my take on existential loneliness in general. And I have often wondered why Peter wanted to work with songs that were so far from the blues tradition he himself identified with. Peter had just returned from England, where he had celebrated international success with blues legend Alexis Korner and his band CCS. Daisy's music was built on European music and had strong symphonic features. Perhaps it was the loneliness of the songs that attracted him without him realizing it? The album was the end of Daisy. We found ourselves at a dead end and it was clear that we had to split up in order to find a way to move forward.

The 70s were coming to an end too, and together with bassist Jacob Perbøll and drummer Jens G Nielsen, I formed the trio Warm Guns, in which I sang and played piano. There wasn't much music in that decade that touched my heart, apart from songs by the Beach Boys, Scott Walker, Badfinger and Stealers Wheel. And then there were Bowie's *Heroes*, produced by Tony Visconti, and Costello's *Armed Forces*, produced by Nick Lowe, both masterpieces in my opinion. And of course, there was ABBA with some amazing hits. ABBA was one of the ensembles that produced some of the most iconic and archetypal pop songs of that strange decade. Yet it was only in the beginning of the 80s that the established and so-called serious bands and songwriters could no longer dismiss the long line of ABBA songs that carried on the tradition of the Beach Boys and Phil Spector, combined with their own Swedish folk musical background, into a new era. It was obvious to me that Benny Anderson and Björn Ulvæus, like Brian Wilson of the Beach Boys and Justin Hayward of the Moody Blues, created music from the heart. There was nothing calculating or cynical behind it, just this devoted and insistent endeavour to create the ultimate pop song that moves people. And with Agnetha Fältskog and Anni-Frid Lyngstad's crisp and compassionate voices, it was only a matter of time before this, in many ways quirky, quartet would find their rightful place in popular music history. The band's first singles, *People Need Love* and *He's My Brother*, served as statements of intent. Therefore, ABBA's success was set in stone from the start. Yet ABBA became the story of the ugly duckling that turns into the most beautiful swan all over again. Even though ABBA had been a swan from the very beginning, it wasn't something the band themselves cared about. Today, everyone recognizes that ABBA's body of work remains a masterclass in pop music from the heart that still moves people around the world. The immediate and heartfelt has always appealed to me more than the intellectually minded.

In 1981 Warm Guns, now with Lars Hybel on guitar and bass, were to record a new album, *Italiano Moderno*, at Eden Studios in London – the studios where Elvis Costello & the Attractions and Nick Lowe & Rockpile recorded. London record label Phonogram had recommended a promising new producer, Rod Houison, so it was with great expectations that Warm Guns entered the legendary studio. After a session listening to the day's work, Rod suddenly pointed to the copy of *What's On in London* I was studying. At the back of the magazine, I had come across a series of adverts offering psychic readings. "Have you ever had one?" Rod asked. "No," I replied, knowing that I had to have one. The address was at the bottom of the advert, so 15 minutes later I was on my way by taxi to the College of Psychic Studies in South Kensington. To my amazement, a long queue of people from all walks of life, including housewives, punks and a couple of classic bowler-clad City businessmen, were lined up outside the beautiful buildings that also housed the Conan Doyle Library. For £2 I bought a ticket for a reading and was shown to the third floor, where a young woman of my own age was waiting for me.

We greeted each other briefly, but I sensed that the woman was not interested in any kind of distracting small talk. She didn't want to know my name or where I was from. All she asked was to be allowed to receive a personal item of mine, as she needed to have an object that belonged to me. Holding my wristwatch, she now started to transmit greetings from my deceased little sister and my grandparents, who were also no longer on the earth plane. Finally, she announced that in a few years I would meet a man who would help me understand how to use my abilities and that I would eventually write a series of books that would affect many people. Finally, she ended the session by telling me that a woman named Sylvia was waiting for me because she had some important information for me regarding my future work.

When I returned to Denmark, my friend, philosopher John Engelbrecht, gave me a picture he told me depicted the

World Mother[14] – an image that was supposedly channelled and physically manifested by three women from the Order of the World Mother. It was exactly at the time I had become interested in Mariam Magdalene and her relationship with Yeshua. When I saw the image of the World Mother, my first thought was that she was a mixture of the Virgin Mary and Mariam Magdalene. The picture followed me in various homes for the next several years, where she stayed always close to me on the wall in my study.

Twenty-two years later, in 2004, I had just finished my book *The Magdalene*, which was about to go to print, when I suddenly saw the picture of the World Mother above my desk. I couldn't believe it. How could I have overlooked her? Of course, she should be on the cover of the book. After a quick call to both the publisher and the printer, I learned that the cover had already been printed, but that the content was on its way to print right now and that it was still possible to get the picture in the back of the book. And so it was.

A few months later, I was on a lecture tour in Denmark in connection with the book release. After a talk in Copenhagen, an elderly gentleman asked: "Where did the picture in the back of the book come from and who does it represent?" I told him that I got the picture from John Engelbrecht and that in my eyes, it was a combined image of both the Virgin Mary and Mary Magdalene.

"Then I think you should meet my mum, Gudrun Ørnsgaard!" he replied resolutely. A week later, I returned

---

[14] The World Mother is an icon representing the essence of all elevated feminine principles and all mythological goddesses, avatars and bodhisattvas such as Ishtar, Isis, Freya, the Virgin Mary and Mary Magdalene. The icon was channelled by three unknown women from the World Mother Order, a French spiritual order for women who undergo various spiritual initiations to enhance clairvoyance, health and healing abilities. The picture also radiates the integrated female and male aspects in one being, which can be recognized when one first places a hand over one half of the face, and then over the other half.

to Copenhagen to meet her. I took the S-train to Charlotten-lund and went straight to Sophus Claussensvej, where Gudrun lived.

"It took you a long time," was her greeting when she opened the door. I looked disorientated at the blue-clad woman, with hat, veil, white lace gloves and pearl wreath, standing in front of me. Hadn't it taken me just a few minutes to walk from the station to her address? Only when I sat across from her in her living room did I begin to realize the magnitude of this encounter. Gudrun told me how, as a young woman at the beginning of World War II, she had found herself in London, where she had married an Englishman. She had just given birth to their son but was not happy. Her husband seemed to have many secrets and Gudrun sensed that he was living a hidden life that she didn't know about. So, she left him. I can't help thinking with admiration of her for choosing to leave a marriage and a home in the midst of the bombings in London. Joining the Mazdaznan movement,[15] Gudrun met some women who helped her find a room and look took care of her son when she worked as a Samaritan among the wounded in the ruins after the bombings. It was through one of the women from the movement that she came into contact with the Order of the World Mother. Only later did her husband tell her that he was working as a secret agent for MI5, but by then it was too late for her to heal the rift between them.

After the war, Gudrun moved to Denmark but attended annual meetings of the Mazdaznan movement in Germany and England until she was contacted by the World Mother Order in 1959 and asked to meet in Montségur, where she and eleven other women were initiated in a secret cave in

---

[15] Mazdaznan is a Neo-Zoroastrian religion that believes that the Earth will be restored to a garden where humanity can co-operate and talk to God. Founded in the late 19th century by Otoman Zar-Adusht Ha'nish, born Otto Hanisch, the religion was a revival of 6th century Mazdakism.

the Montségur mountain. Afterwards, each of the women were taken to one of the so-called Cathar castles, where they spent three days. But there wasn't a castle for Gudrun – being the youngest of all the women, she was the last to be considered and was taken to the Church of Mary Magdalene in Rennes-le-Chateau.

After three days there, she was picked up by the Order's Moon Priestess and was given responsibility for the image of the World Mother. And it was at this point in Gudrun's story that I suddenly understood who she was. The moon priestess, who was French and gave Gudrun the precious icon, was unable to pronounce Gudrun's name and therefore used her other name, Sylvia.

Sylvia! Here she was, sitting in a living room in Charlottenlund, pointing to a stack of papers. "If you hadn't come now, I would have had to burn the treasures hidden there. I was informed that you were coming several years ago, so you can understand that I was getting rather impatient."

This was the start of a friendship that lasted until Sylvia's death on 1 January 2016. It was Sylvia who introduced me to the insights of the esoteric wedding of the inner feminine and masculine principles based on her interpretation of the Grail myth: "If you want to find the princess, you must first find the dragon that holds her captive and then slay it. It is the responsibility of every Grail knight to undertake this task." Later I realized that the dragon symbolized my own inner shadows, while the princess was a metaphor for the feminine principle in me. Only by recognizing and transforming these shadows can the feminine be released.

In the same way, she told me, every woman must acknowledge the presence of an inner dragon before her masculine principle/the Grail knight can emerge and free her feminine principle/the princess from the shadow sides of her personality.

Shortly before Sylvia's death, I visited her while she was already in the phase of transitioning between worlds.

She was loudly channelling information from the World of Answers into the Earth plane until the very end. The connection between Sylvia and me was deeply rooted in past lives. In the current incarnation, we had an intuitive contact with each other that meant I always sensed when she wanted me to call. She would always answer the phone with: "You're learning," followed by her unmistakable, tinkling laugh.

6

THE KINGDOM OF HEAVEN

How sweet the sound, within and around

In 1988 I found Dr Edith R Stauffer's ground-breaking book *Unconditional Love and Forgiveness*. It was especially the subtitle, *The Essene Precepts and their Contemporary Value*, that immediately attracted me. Dr Stauffer was the director of Psychosynthesis International at the time. She was a student of the founder of psychosynthesis, Dr Roberto Assagioli, MD, in Florence and had also visited the Martinus Institute in Copenhagen.

The book includes an English translation of the original Aramaic version of the *Sermon on the Mount* from the *Gospel of Matthew* in the New Testament, which Stauffer traced back to fragment 4Q525 of the Dead Sea Scrolls. The content of the fragment points to a clear connection between Yeshua and the Essenes:

"Blessed are the pure in heart who speak no untruth.

Blessed are those who observe the commandments of Wisdom and do no evil.

Blessed are those who delight in her and shun the ways of folly.

Blessed are those who seek her with pure intent and are not restrained by a hardened heart."

In Chapter 19 (Aramaic Cornerstones) you can find Stauffer's interpretation of the Sermon on the Mount based on her knowledge of the Aramaic language, which was the language Yeshua and his contemporaries spoke. I immediately realized that this was the language I had been looking for, but that it was not just a matter of translating this language – it was crucial to know the psychology behind it.

The origin of Aramaic is not known, only that it is 3,000 years old and the mother of Hebrew and Arabic. I once asked a Syrian priest from the Syrian Orthodox Church, which uses Aramaic as a liturgical language, if he could tell me where it came from. "It was brought to Earth by Angels so that we humans have a language with which we are able to talk to God," he replied with a big smile.

Nowadays Aramaic is only spoken in very few places on the Earth. In its children – Hebrew and Arabic – we can find the same deeper layer of transformational psychology and mystical wisdom that constitutes the essence of Aramaic, although this is unbeknown to most Jews and Arabs. Among the Jews, usually only the rabbis are aware of the divine psychology behind the language as a tool to gaining a deeper understanding of the religious scriptures; for the Arabs, the Sufis are the keepers of this sacred knowledge.

I wrote to Edith Stauffer to find out where I could study Aramaic. She sent me photocopies with selected passages of the *Khaboris Manuscript*, an Aramaic New Testament believed to be a copy of an original New Testament that was the basis for the first Greek translations. Today, the earliest New Testament we use is written in Greek, but we know that a long line of early Church fathers: Ephihanius, St Jerome, Papias, Origen, Eusebius and Clement of Alexandria, to name a few, all referred to and often quoted from an original Aramaic scripture called *The Gospel of the Nazareens*. This gospel later became known as *The Aramaic Gospel According to Matthew*.

It was among the photocopies Edith Stauffer sent me that I found the answer to a question that had haunted me for a long time: What was the meaning of the term *Kingdom of Heaven* that Yeshua said was within us? In no other languages beside Aramaic, Hebrew and Arabic, be it Danish, English, French, Italian, etcetera, is it possible to understand the concept and its meaning through the term itself. No wonder the vast majority of people are not aware of this crucial part of Yeshua's teachings, because they have never been introduced to it – not even in the churches that should have been the natural place of sharing such essential knowledge.

The Kingdom of Heaven Within

Aramaic, like most languages, is based on so-called root words. However, Aramaic root words seem to differ from the root words in other languages. An Aramaic root can carry up to eight different meanings that can even seem to be contradictory to each other. So in order to translate a word in Aramaic, we must see the overall continuum of meanings for this word and find or create a term in our language that would hold the essence of this particular word. The so-called *midrash* tradition, which is as old as the Aramaic language, is a translation/understanding tool that seeks just such an essence.

It is important to know that each letter in the Aramaic language represents a divine quality or creational force, so a vast variety of qualities or frequencies can be expressed through combinations of the two, three or four letters within a root word. Before working with Aramaic concepts in our spiritual practice it is very helpful to integrate the understanding that we are opening doors to powerful cosmic principles by placing our focus on even one letter, let alone a whole word, which can be rightly seen as a universe of frequencies.

One of the most transformational and healing Aramaic concepts is *Malkoota d'Shmeya* – The Kingdom of Heaven. In the term *Malkoota* we find the root word *MLK* (kingdom, royal, exalted) with the added suffix "-oota". In Aramaic syntax this suffix turns the concept of the word into an expression for an active human behaviour or judgement. Consequently, if we think or speak the word *Malkoota*, we invite an "exalted" or heightened field of consciousness into our awareness and we will experience a shift of frequency in our Light Body that is activating change in our own behaviour or in the circumstances of our everyday life.

In *d'Shmeya*, which translates as *heavenly*, we find the root word *SHM*. *SHM* means *name; identity; sound; vibration; light/consciousness; clarity; expression; manifestation; God's identity and image (I AM), consciousness or essence in humans.* We carry the essence of Heaven right within us! And, even more excitingly, the suffix "*-eya*" means *that which can never cease* or *that which is eternal*. When we voice *d'Shmeya*, we therefore activate the individualized God Consciousness that we *are*, the divine seed within us that will never cease to flourish, the unshakable clarity, the eternal frequency of Union and Harmony.

Within the depths of the Aramaic language, we can find a very beautiful image in which a root word is compared with a human being. Both carry the essence of the truth and eternity of what they are ready to express within themselves but are in need of an activation. The Aramaic word/concept *Ephatah* is another example of such an activation. The meaning of the root *PHTH* is the possibility to open something. With the added suffix "*-tah*", the word transforms into an activated field of healing. As we know from the *Gospel of Mark*, Yeshua used it as a command when he was healing: *Ephatah! Be opened!* An even wider understanding of the word *Ephatah* would include an interpretation of the letter *E* and the ending *ah, E* being an expansion of the letter *Alif*, which represents the Creator, the mover, the penetrator or the commander, and *ah* depicting the breath that animates something.

It is always inspiring for me to find similar principles in different traditions. The Aramaic concept of *SHM* is identical to the concept of *Shabd*[16] from the Sant Mat tradition, which originated in India in the 13th century and is based on the oldest Vedic and Sufi traditions. About *Shabd*, Huzur Maharaj Sawan Singh writes in *Philosophy of the Masters*:

"*Shabd* is a Sanskrit word. Its original root is not known. It means sound, letter, voice, name, conscience, word, clarity, declaration, expression, speech, etc. That which can be spoken or that which can reveal secrets, is called *Shabd*. However, the Gurus and the highest Masters have used it in a very deep and abstruse sense.

Before the creation, the *Shabd* was unmanifested and nameless. It then existed in itself. In that state it was called indescribable, nameless, invisible, un-fathomable, unutterable and inexpressible. When it became manifest it became known as *Nam* or *Shabd*.

'When *Shabd* was unmanifested it had no name. When *Shabd* manifested, it became the Name.'

Prior to it becoming manifest, there was no sun or moon or sky. The *Shabd* was formless. The *Shabd*, however, is consciousness. All are under its control. Nothing can manifest without its help. The *Shabd* is the life, the essence, the root and the quintessence of every created thing. It does not depend on any one for manifestation. On the other hand, all that is manifest or unmanifest is sustained by it.

The *Shabd*, Sound Current, Word or Holy Spirit is not a subject matter for speech or writing. In order

---

[16] Both *SHM* and *Shabd* begin with the two letters *Sh*, which according to the Kabbalistic tradition is the sound of the Holy Spirit. It is the 21st letter *Shin* in the Aramaic/Hebrew alphabet and expresses the driving force behind all creation. *Sh* can also be found in the Aramaic/Hebrew term *Shekinah*, meaning 'the majestic presence and manifestation of God'. *Shekinah* was the spirit of God that hovered over the waters before everything was created. This water is a metaphor for the womb waters of a pregnant woman. *Shekinah* is God's radiance and manifesting power in the physical world.

to make it understood, we can only say this much, namely that it is the quintessence of the Lord and that it sustains millions of universes and regions. It is the soul-current of consciousness. It is the Celestial Melody. It is the life-current which originates from the Lord and pervades everything. The Lord creates and sustains the entire universe through this great Current of Power. It gives life to the whole of the creation and can take every living being back to his Original Home or the Lord. The currents of the Lord pervade everywhere, like radio-waves. His divine music fills all space. Unless we are correctly tuned to it, we cannot hear this music. As we grow more and more subtle, we begin to hear clearly its melodies. *Shabd* is a string which connects everyone and everything with the Lord.

The *Shabd* is the basis of all true religions, for religion means that which connects us with the Lord. All the forces of nature are sustained by the *Shabd*. The life force is also its manifestation, even though it is working in the regions of Maya. Like electricity, *Shabd*, whether manifest or unmanifest, pervades everywhere. It is all-powerful and is the Creator of all."

The *Shabd* or *SHM* is the principle within us that is forever our connecting link home to our starting point: God or Divine Consciousness. It is the activating principle in God's Light and Consciousness that cannot pass away. It is the Eternal Power or Holy Spirit within us.

The Kingdom of Heaven/*Malkoota d'Shmeya* is a field of consciousness that we can access through the understanding and awareness of the *SHM/Shabd*. Within this field, we perceive and feel a connection to all people, all beings and all visible and invisible realities.

And when we "look" into another human being or see their true nature, it is *SHM* (God Consciousness) that we see and communicate with. *SHM* is the seed from which everything in our lives is manifested, as well as the cosmic current of all creation. And whatever is in the seed is also in the tree that grows from it. *SHM* is the manifesting force and all creation is the effect of it. Whatever is present in the cause is also present in the effect. Through this understanding we know that we are all children of God.

The fifth element

This book is about the ether and its importance to humans. Different researchers of Spiritual Science have received different systems and terms in regard to the multiple layers within the etheric and astral realms. To me and my own experimental explorations, it is impossible to determine where one layer ends and the next begins. But there is one common denominator that matters the most to me, as it unites all individual experiences from all research: reality beyond the physical world IS.

I use the term *ether* to describe all layers of reality beyond the physical. The part of the ether closest to the physical world and the human body is the slowest pulsating frequency, while the upper layers are the fastest pulsating frequencies. Due to these different frequencies, the entire ether continuum acts partly as a veil and partly as a connecting medium between worlds. The whole idea of parallel universes that are not separate, but are folded into each other, helps us to understand the Essene teaching that has been passed on to us in their writings: *what is here is also there* and vice versa. Consequently, the etheric continuum is always available to us as long as we have the password. And the password is spiritual practice. It is part of our spiritual commitment to find the practice that each one of us can best communicate through.

To most people it is through prayer, invocation and meditation that we connect to the ether, which contains the information we usually seek through other means, but which is activated and opens up when we dedicate ourselves to God Consciousness – the One Infinite Source, the Heavenly Origin, the Universal Intelligence behind all creation. When we understand that NOTHING can exist without being infused with God Consciousness, a whole new realm of realization opens up and the foundation is laid for us to truly break through the ego's wall of ignorance that leads to all separation. We can now glimpse freedom on the other side. A freedom that has always been there, we were just not able to see it. Until now!

The ether is the fifth element, which contains a multitude of layers, of which *SHM* is the most potent. Most people know the expression: "We're on air!" – a phrase that is still used by broadcasters when a station sends out sound and images to listeners and viewers. It's a natural expression that we have long since accepted. But few people think about how it is possible to transmit sound and images through "the air", and that the sound and images can be heard and seen almost immediately on various receivers, even though the signals have travelled hundreds or even thousands of kilometres without us being able to see the transmitted content passing by through the air or even a movement of the waves in the ether with the naked eye.

However, it is thought-provoking and symptomatic of the limitations we humans find ourselves in that we find it hard to accept that we – who invented radio and TV transmission and reception devices – are not ourselves capable of consciously sending and receiving signals. Because that's what we humans do – transmit and receive – whether we are aware of this or not.

The ether is a conductive element that carries electrical impulses and signals. As mentioned, the ether is divided into different frequency ranges, and it is crucial to know on which frequencies the different degrees of electricity and consciousness are travelling. The ether consists of a luminous web of consciousness, certain qualities and a universal Law of Light, which is the unifying force that allows the web and all creation to exist. The fastest frequency of the ether, *SHM*, is the gateway in which a transition to higher dimensions can take place. The active force that constitutes the password to this gateway is what in Judaism and Christianity is called Spirit, in Aramaic *Rukha*.

Once humankind realizes that the ethereal *SHM* Light Grid offers the endless and free form of energy – which Nikola Tesla, among others, was on the trail of – and which is the driving force that makes it possible for beings from other star systems to travel light years in an earthly instant, humanity will take a new step on the ladder of evolution. *SHM* is the only never-ceasing fuel in existence.

The multiverse and its energies

The multiverse consists of a number of non-physical dimensions beyond the spectrum of time and space from which humans in the physical world receive visions, images and information. This happens most often and for most people in dreams at night when we sleep. The Light Beings/ non-physical consciousnesses that inhabit these non-physical worlds are able to materialize and dematerialize in the physical world and have done so since the beginning of time. Some of these Beings are the Angels described in the Bible and the Book of Enoch, which are Beings of Light who serve various creative and life-sustaining purposes and are thus able to manifest themselves wherever they are needed.

This is where ancient mystery traditions such as the Essenes of Mount Carmel, Heliopolis and Damascus, and the Therapists of Alexandria in Egypt come in. The people associated with these mystery schools were called healers and mystics. A mystic is a person who, unlike today's scientists, uses himself/herself as an experimental centre. Whereas scientists study the measurable physical outside of themselves and believe that their mindset and conscious and unconscious expectation have no influence in the process of observation, the mystic starts any research with the focus on the spiritual realm within. The mystics of the ancient mystery schools knew that the *SHM* Light Grid in the ether is one of the most important gateways to the collective God Consciousness, and they knew the password.

It is this *SHM* frequency, that gives access to the Book of Life mentioned in the *Book of Revelation,* that Edgar Cayce also frequented, in which everything humans have thought, felt, said and done since the beginning of time is stored. It is from here that the long line of ideas, solutions and visions that flow to people who seriously work to promote true peace and health and find new genuine solutions to humanity's problems, originate.

Insight through such access will one day bring about a revolution in all areas of human life on Earth. All our current technological inventions, devices and gadgets, fossil fuels, etcetera, will be completely obsolete from one moment to the next. Any form of physical transport will take place through our expanded awareness and knowledge of nonlocality.

The concept of nonlocality covers the interactive connection of all beings and everything with each other. It includes the fact that every feeling, thought and intention a human being has is immediately present everywhere and that to move from one place to another, all we need to do is, through visualization and intention, direct our entire being in the direction we want to go. We will then understand that physical reality is not the only one, but that there is an infinity of parallel universes and that moving from one universe to another is not separated by a barrier of time or space, because time as we perceive it today is only a temporary and apparent reality.

There are other beings that visit us solely through the power of thought, without the use of physical means of transport. By mastering presence, intention and visualization, such beings become one with whoever or whatever they wish to communicate with and can be in several places at once. This is how nonlocality and bilocation work. Recent observations suggest that there are beings that only teleport themselves as pure Light in the form of so-called orbs, through which they are able to manifest themselves wherever they want to travel. We humans, too, are always in several places at once, but mostly without being aware of it. We will understand who we truly are when we become aware of our ability to bypass time and space. Many people know the feeling of walking right next to themselves. That's why we often feel like we never quite succeed at anything or keep a clear focus or get a grip on what we believe we really want to achieve.

When we realize that we have always already arrived because we are one with everything, unimaginable perspectives open up for the individual and humanity. Our higher Self (expressed through the I AM) exists solely in the Now and does not relate to references such as past and future. The myth of the fall of the Angels is about humanity's fall from this higher Self to the small self, the ego, which Yeshua and the Essenes referred to as "satan".

Just as *Heaven* in Aramaic is first and foremost an expression of an inner state of heightened consciousness, the concept of *hell* is also an expression of a state: it indicates that we are beside ourselves, that we are out of balance and therefore unable to fulfil our purpose in the incarnation.

Hell is therefore directly related to the Aramaic concept of *kheetha,* which is usually translated as "sin", but actually means "to err" or "to miss the mark". Like an archer who misses his target. What do we do when we are not able to hit the mark or to succeed? We step closer to the target and try again. This time with more attention. In its essence, the word *kheetha* or sin therefore means failure due to lack of presence. And presence cannot be degraded by anyone or anything! Only our own will or focus is responsible for us to be more or less present, vibrate higher or lower, live and act with more or less awareness and compassion.

When we circumvent the Law of Light, we are not present. Presence cannot be faked. Presence means that we are able to listen. Listen to our true voice within. Listen in everyday life to someone other than ourselves. It means not interrupting the other person while they are in the middle of an explanation, just because you need to get your own story off your chest.

Presence is being able to become one with other people, situations, animals and nature. Presence is being able to move and accomplish what you feel called to do without always needing the attention of others or confirmation that you are good enough. True presence therefore presupposes that you are able to rest in yourself and neither need to puff yourself up nor hide away. You simply ARE present in participatory listening. You listen to both your inner voice as well as everything that is happening around you.

Presence means never referring to someone who is standing next to us in the third person. If we do, we immediately create noise and separation. And separation is the opposite of presence.

Presence is being fully and one hundred per cent aware and compassionately present. From here, a silent prayer can enter into our being, and we are stepping into the conscious space of "knocking" that Yeshua has invited us to. And through our listening and presence the door to our higher Self will be opened. We are therefore masters of which higher worlds and levels of consciousness we can reach, through a renewed and authentic behaviour and attitude. We must never forget that everywhere we go we bring our version of the Kingdom of Heaven with us, and that we are on a path toward aligning ourselves totally with God Consciousness. Remember: a kingdom that is not aligned with its true purpose cannot stand.

7

PROPHECY AND REBIRTH

Children of the Sky ... it's time to ally

In the following years, I intensified my studies of Aramaic, which led to the opening I had been waiting for to manifest. Along the way, I moved to the small island of Samsø with my girlfriend at the time. We were both at a point in our lives where we needed a change and a lot of silence. Samsø was the right place for us. I said goodbye to touring but continued to write songs and music. My first books were written on Samsø in 1992. These included the book *Zoé*, which was not only a novel, but a total liberation of conscious writing, a complete surrender to intuition and its inscrutable ways, which gave rise to a text that in hindsight feels like a prophecy – and which also became the indirect reason why I came into contact with my teacher, the Seer Calle Montségur, some years later.

Zoé was the first of my books in which I surrendered unconditionally to whatever lay hidden in my sub-consciousness. Every morning for a few months, I began my day at five by writing down everything that flowed freely from a place inside me that I later realized was a kind of mystical cauldron in which etheric information was gathered and released at that time because I was ready to receive it. It was literally a stream of consciousness process in which I was not only the writer, but also the reader or traveller in the book, looking forward each day to where the journey would take me. The book determined its own direction. It is the "easiest" of my books, precisely because I was not called upon to think, but simply wrote down the sentences exactly as they came. To me, it is therefore an extremely important book, and when I read it afterwards, it was like reading a book written by another person.

Today, I realize that the book is a deep dive into my incarnational past and future, as well as a vessel in which a series of prophecies have been collected. Some of them are closer to our current reality than it might be comfortable to think about. I am aware how fine the line is between writing down a vision or recalling a past life incident and playing a part in a re-creation of a similar situation in this lifetime, as our focus creates frequencies and frequencies lead to manifestations. We carry the responsibility for our creations, and even more so if we share them, as we release them into the collective conscious awareness. In the following you will find a quote from the book, the description of a past event that at the time foreshadowed a future encounter. The encounter with Calle.

Zoé was given to Calle Montségur by a friend of mine, the singer-songwriter and author Pia Raug, three years before our paths would be crossing. It was that book that made Calle recognize me and realize that he and I should work together. But he also knew that everything had to happen in the right order, and so he waited for my phone call that morning when, in a last desperate attempt to find a way out of my stagnated state, I called him for his help. It was the following passage from the book that convinced him that he and I were destined for each other.

The book's first-person narrator is crossing the Pyrenees into Spain when he is captured by the Inquisition, who tortures him to get information about the Cathars in France:

"Yes, he had met a stranger. They were right about that. But he had never in his life met a person like this stranger. He had never heard a person speak so simply and understandably about such incomprehensible things. The words that came out of this man's mouth hit him right in the centre of his heart, right where the blood dripped from all the new, incomprehensible things that had been so fateful for him, but which had also in some unfathomable way given him hope for another life, for breaking through the fatal horizon. The man's words had brought him into a state of rest that he could not remember having experienced since his earliest childhood. Like when a mother breastfeeds her child and the child falls asleep in her arms, full and tired.

'Perfect', the man had said, 'Perfect!'"

After the episode in the Pyrenees, the book's hero continues his travels toward the Alhambra.

This was written three years before I got in touch with Calle Montségur and he asked me to come to Montségur in the Pyrenees. The book expressed a psychic/etheric field I had reached that had strong personal and collective indications. Immediately after the book was published in 1995, a shift occurred in my physical and psychological state that put me out of action from one day to the next and resulted in three years where I was bedridden for longer and longer periods. There is no doubt in my mind that this condition was due to the fact that I had come into contact with a parallel universe or one or more past lives through my work with *Zoé*, which means "life" in Greek, and that I was carrying around some themes or remnants that needed to be transformed. My lack of insight into how to integrate these energetic resonances was the direct cause of me having to go through three years of hell. I was tossed into different episodes of pain, in which I felt being pierced by a spear that had entered from the neck right through my heart. The constant, almost unbearable dizziness filled me with fear of leaving the bed that seemed to move like a ship under me. Sometimes, driven by a terrible sickness, I was able to scrape together enough strength and courage to crawl out of my bed into the bathroom where I would be sick, lying on the cold bathroom floor afterwards in a short relief of total exhaustion.

After visiting a number of doctors, specialists and alternative practitioners, I realized that no one was able to diagnose my symptoms, let alone suggest a treatment. A week before I connected with Calle, the following happened. After three years of spending far too much time in bed, feeling like I was standing at the bottom of a mud hole, trying to get a firm grip on the edge of reality above me, crawling my way up, until I almost reached it, but each time I was about to make it, my strength left me and I fell back into the mud, giving in to despair and exhaustion until I was ready to creep around again, one day an inner voice sounded.

It said: "Since you are lying here in such pain, why don't you take on the pain of all the sufferers of the world so that you suffer for them. Then your otherwise meaningless condition will at least have a purpose?"

It may sound like megalomania, but in that moment, I knew that there was only one answer for me: Yes! And immediately, the condition transformed. I couldn't get out of bed, but I felt that the pain was neutralized. Something had changed. Now I was just waiting for the final step. It came the following week when I connected with Calle, who after a brief exchange on the phone told me that from now until we would meet six months later, I should not worry, everything would fall into place. Five minutes after the call, I felt an energetic activity around my head followed by a slight throbbing in my neck (medulla oblongata), which caused intense fatigue. After an hour of deep sleep, I woke up and could immediately feel a significant difference. Three years of black and white had suddenly turned into a world of the deepest and most beautiful colours. All sounds were crystal clear. I felt like I was born again.

Could this be the rebirth Yeshua spoke of in the *Gospel of John*, Chapter 3:1-13?

"There was a man, one of the Pharisees, named Nicodemus, a member of the Sanhedrin. He came to Yeshua at night and said to him: 'Rabbi, we know that you are a teacher come from God; for no one can do the signs that you do unless God is with him.' Yeshua answered him: 'Truly, truly, I say to you: he who is not born again cannot see the kingdom of God.' Nicodemus said to him: 'How can a man be born when he is old? Surely he cannot enter his mother's womb a second time and be born?' Yeshua answered: 'Verily, verily, I say unto thee: whoever is not born of water and the Spirit cannot enter the kingdom of God. That which is born of the flesh is flesh, and that which is born of the Spirit is spirit. Do not be surprised that I said to you: you must be born again. The wind blows wherever it pleases, and you hear it blowing, but you do not know where it comes from or where it is going. So it is with everyone who is born of the Spirit.'

Nicodemus asked him: 'How can this be?' Yeshua replied: 'You are a teacher in Israel and do not understand? Truly, truly, I say to you: we speak of what we know and we testify of what we have seen, but you do not accept our testimony. If you do not believe when I speak to you of earthly things, how will you believe when I speak to you of heavenly things? No one has ascended into heaven except the one who descended from heaven, the Son of Man.'"

Who is this "Son/Daughter of Man" Yeshua refers to? It is every incarnate human being who has come to realize their true origin and therefore now takes responsibility for all that this awareness entails. By midlife (ages 48–52), we have usually come to terms with some of the ambitions we thought life was about. When we are born into the world, we are welcomed by well-meaning people, our parents, who want the best for us. They try to guide us and teach us the game of life. It's about making something of ourselves, which usually means gaining the respect of other people, achieving high social status and surrounding ourselves with material signs that we have done well. Unfortunately, such a journey often means that the spiritual aspects in us are forgotten and receive no attention. In my case, the connection to this side of me had been mainly an intellectual one. I hadn't spent much time on spiritual practice, while I studied the world religions and especially Christian mysticism and now also the Aramaic language. But I always knew that, as time went on, I would have to cross the threshold into a life more focused on practice, I just kept putting it off. And when you don't want to hear, you have to feel! There was no doubt that these three years were my "dark night of the soul" that I had now finally come out the other side of and that my redeemer was this seer and naturopath, Calle Montségur.

There is a time for everything. If we stay aware and awake, the eternal now will enfold in a string of moments that will guide us to always be at the right place at the right time. If we miss a moment, the Aramaic saying is that the fruit is rotten (bisha). This is the concept we in the West understand as evil. When the fruit is ready and ripe (tubw), it is good and should be picked NOW. But not before either. If you pick it too early, the fruit is unripe and inedible. That's why presence is such an important state that must be cultivated. It is through presence that we become one with life and experience being in perfect unity with our task and understand when we should step in or pass by.

8

THE GREATEST GIFT

**Now and forever, stupid or clever,
big or small – just call**

In life, coincidence does not exist. Rather, life consists of an infinite series of synchronicities that, when we are aware of them, make it possible to understand our interconnectedness with other people and all living beings.

Everything we do, all of our actions, thoughts and emotions are like seeds that are planted, germinate and later suddenly emerge as potent opportunities or unmanageable challenges, without us necessarily understanding the context that led to their appearances. The moment we are aware of how and why synchronized experiences take place, life is filled with meaning of a previously unknown nature. And it is in the realization that this expanded experience of everyday life is only possible because life is infused with *Rukha d'Koodsha* (Holy Spirit), providing wholeness through the interconnectedness of all individuals, that we can rightly say we are gifted. It is not *Rukha d'Koodsha* that is the gift, but our ability to be or become aware of its ubiquitous presence.

Rukha d'Koodsha is an expression of a form of ethereal intelligence that, through its activity and our recognition of it, generates gracefulness, generosity and gratitude.

Here are two examples from everyday life that illustrate how the Holy Spirit can work. Recently, Naleea and I were in Glastonbury for a workshop and concert. One morning, we had some time off and spent it in one of the town's well-stocked bookshops. Suddenly, a woman approaches me and asks if I would be "the famous healer from YouTube". I give her a puzzled look and reply that I'm not. The woman apologizes and remarks that I look exactly like this healer before she leaves the bookstore.

After a while, Naleea notes that I may have misunderstood the woman: she might not have described me the way I would perceive myself, but she surely has meant me. I immediately engage in a rapid inner dialogue, shifting from a variety of thoughts into an uneasy feeling about myself. As we leave the store, I observe myself diving from judgemental remorse to transformative thoughts and back again. Once on the street, we are deeply engaged in a conversation about how small everyday episodes like this can lead to painful misunderstandings. I tell Naleea that I wish I could talk to the woman again so I could correct my mistake – my lack of being present, that could be perceived as a lack of care. I have just uttered the words when we practically bump into the woman. I explain the context of the situation to her, and we exchange warm expressions and a heartfelt goodbye that leaves me with a deep sense of gratitude that my wish was heard and granted. This example may not seem like a big deal. But I felt it as the most precious gift. To be given an opportunity to right a wrong makes my heart wide, and my spirit soar.

Most people are familiar with experiencing "coincidences", such as calling someone who is already on the phone because both parties dialled each other's number at the same time. Or thinking about someone you haven't seen or heard from in ten or twenty years and then suddenly receiving a phone call from them. Last year, Daisy reunited. While I was writing a small book about the history of the band, I was reminded of a young girl about 15 years old from my hometown whom I met after one of the band's concerts in 1971. We spent the rest of the evening and night immersed in conversation. It was clear that we both experienced a deep recognition and veneration in the meeting. As the sun appeared, we walked toward the suburb where I lived. There we said goodbye and she headed for her home. I never saw nor heard from her again. Now, after more than 40 years, she suddenly reappeared in my thoughts.

The next day, I received an email from this "young girl", who was now a grown woman, married and living in Canada with her husband, children and grandchildren. She told me that immediately after our meeting she had gone on an Inter Rail trip through Europe. One day, she had been attacked by a group of young guys but had been rescued by a Canadian man whom she later married and was still with.

These are just two of countless examples I have experienced in my life. We are actually able to attract somebody's attention just by sending positive thoughts toward a person through the ether. And just like in the second incident, the "call" will be picked up and answered.

In the Russian and Greek Orthodox tradition, monks invoke the Holy Spirit in a very simple way, like it is the most normal and natural relationship in the world. They don't question or doubt that it is manifested, once they call for it. They know that it is always present, but that it is activated through their conscious recognition of it. We just need to ask ourselves: what intentions underlie our thoughts or desires? What do we want to achieve through the presence and action of the Holy Spirit? There are no situations that are more important, greater or lesser than others, so we can call it into any and all of our daily tasks, projects and meetings. However, if we harbour negative motives, we create noise instead of harmony, and our Guardian Angel, the etheric helper associated with our etheric Light Body, intervenes and helps us to understand our error.

Every thought, intention and illness can be read in the human auric field that makes up the Light Body. A person who constantly entertains negative thoughts will darken the aura, weaken the functions and organs of the body and create a distance to other people who will try to avoid dwelling in the energy that radiates from such a person. One of the most common human disorders today is the absence of presence.

We can find the cause in a multitude of factors in our way of living today. Take our technological and industrialized society, for example. The technical, medical and social developments of the last decades have meant that we live longer. Most of us are not burdened with hard physical work, we have almost immediate access to an abundance of products and information. But our bodies and psyches have to deal with fluoride in our drinking water, poor nutrition with artificial and often toxic additives, a rise of depression and anxiety through the decline of communal living, a reduced contact with the relaxing and healing environment of nature and more and more screen time, often experienced with excessive negative emotions triggered by contents of crime, war, fraud, hatred and violence.

All of these factors have a direct numbing effect on all of the human spiritual and metaphysical faculties, creating, at worst, spiritual insensibility, apathy, separation and dissolution. It is not the single violent film or the single piece of nitrite sausage that kills or desensitizes us, but the sum total of violent films and nitrite-containing foods together that slowly does so.

Therefore, the first step toward detoxification is to be more aware of exactly what we are filling ourselves with physically, mentally/intellectually and spiritually. Everything is connected. Through sustained meditation, contemplation and prayer, we can dissolve numbness and reconnect with the God Consciousness within us. No show, however colourful, or no impressive AI-generated work can surpass our inherent human access to eternity with all its infinite possibilities for the evolution of consciousness. And when we open our eyes and realize what an amazing reality awaits us behind all the noise and darkness we have produced over countless centuries, we will first be shocked and then rejoice with rapture and gratitude that it was possible to break the curse.

Millions of people, atheists or believers of different faiths, who have found themselves in a life-threatening situation and as a last resort have prayed to God, the Virgin Mary or Jesus, have experienced a total change in their condition, have been healed or uplifted to such an extent that their lives have subsequently taken a completely new and more meaningful course.

Behold! The time has come to transform ignorance. It starts with a prayer we pray for others, the blessing we send toward someone, or the hand we reach out right now to another person or another country who needs our support. Never to promote or sustain war, but to make peace. Children need our presence, our care and our patience. We in turn need their openness and immediate trust, their welcoming curiosity and playful wisdom.

Most people respond to ethereal energy, but as I said, usually without being aware of what it is that moves them. In relationships, physical attraction is one thing, intellectual attraction another, but there is an overarching attraction on a spiritual level. If physical attraction stands alone, it is usually an erotic, passionate energy that often puts us in a kind of free fall because we put everything else aside to fulfil our desires. Intellectual attraction is often conditioned by control and linked to the ego's need to appear as something extraordinarily desirable. Spiritual attraction arrives with a conscious or unconscious recognition of the soul frequency of the other. It is like a blessing that permeates the meeting of two equally developed souls with its omnipresent Light. It sees the other person in their entirety and at eye level. It is an expression of a deep intuitive connection that links two people to each other. Often these are reincarnational relationships where the people involved have many incarnations in common. The energy that radiates from each of these forms of attraction is different in nature. This is why a quick infatuation can prove disastrous because those involved confuse lust with love. A relationship without an awareness of the higher purpose of the relationship usually has a poor chance of developing. To me, love is first and foremost a wake-up call from the ego's ignorance, numbness and fear.

When all three types of attraction are present in a relationship, it offers possibilities that go beyond the ordinary. The ethereal energy at play between two people who both move on the same high frequency can be read in the ether around them and affects most people who come into contact with them.

When I started seeing luminous crystal formations around other people, I quickly realized that these told me something about a person's current state. Thus, a person's crystal formations differed from one day to the next. But I have learned that energy is expressed in many different ways. Normally, as an individual, we can feel and sense something, without being able to explain what it is. When we get more experienced and accustomed to working with energy, we begin to know how to differentiate between its varying forms of frequencies. But you have to be willing to let go of any kind of judgement and step out of the small and constricting squares of the ego. We must be able to rise above any drama, any insult, any attack and see a situation, ourselves and other people from a higher perspective. Then, every now and again, some ethereal indications reveal themselves that can open the heart and allow us to see God Consciousness in everything, instead of the distorted version of reality we have made our truth. We begin to see, because with *Rukha d'Koodsha's* help we dissolve all forms of fear, judgement and any other mental or emotional noise.

In his book *Clairvoyant Investigations of Christian Origins and Ceremonial,* seer Geoffrey Hodson describes how various church ceremonies, such as the Lord's Supper, when it is given and received with true devotion and presence, activate or invoke Angelic Beings of Light that appear in the ether around those involved in the Eucharist. Many people are able to sense when something so extraordinary is occurring, but without realizing what this extraordinariness really is. Something is shifting in the atmosphere. We feel more peaceful or positive, clarified and refreshed. Most people who have been part of a group that has toned together, i.e., making sound with the voice in free harmony with each other, have felt how the sound suddenly seems to multiply, as if there are invisible voices singing along. I have experienced the participation and presence of such Light Beings every time we sing together in concerts or workshops. I am aware that these Beings are always present, but only seem to be notable or somehow activated as tangible energy when our unified intentions and realizations are released and have a positive and higher purpose than just performance.

Yeshua and the Essenes knew the power of *Rukha d'Koodsha*, how it can be recognized and invoked. The same is possible for us. But it requires us to invest the time it takes for each of us to build a stable and constant connection to this power and live with it as a reality. Chapter 18 provides inspiration for those who don't know where to begin, including the most simple and powerful prayer, which I myself use daily on inhalation and exhalation: *Rukha d'Koodsha – Malkoota d'Shmeya*. In English: *Holy Spirit* (on inhalation) – *Kingdom of Heaven* (on exhalation).

9

THE HAND AND HEART OF YESHUA

**Oh flower! There's a shadow on the meadow.
Rise and run, towards the sun**

In the six months leading up to meeting Calle, I felt like a super-vital plant that kept putting out new shoots. I quit smoking, which had caused me a lot of problems before. Now it happened without struggle or side effects. Wherever I went, I found that strangers would stop me on the street, wanting to talk. On the ferry or the train, toddlers came running up and hugged my legs, even dogs sat faithfully at my feet. I was flooded with a force unknown to me until then, which I attributed to Calle's intervention into my Light Body.

Later, when I was staying with him as his apprentice and co-worker I began to understand the spiritual and metaphysical principles that make up human reality. Sometimes we wake up in the morning with the feeling of not being at home in our own skin. We step out into the world and realize that no one is drawn to us, no one sees us or comes to meet us, no one calls us and maybe even acquaintances and friends wouldn't notice and greet us on the street.

When we try to make contact ourselves, the attempt fails and runs into nothing. We are invisible. That's when our Light Body sits close to the physical body, when it is without energy and radiance.

Other times we wake up feeling comfortable and at rest within ourselves. This is when the Light Body radiates: "Here I am! I am connected and full of inspirational energy!" We have charisma and other people are drawn to us – they seek us out, call us and not only greet us, but embrace us because they sense the life-giving and creative force pulsing around us. This was the state I was in for six months after my recovery, until I met Calle. When I started working with Calle, I learned how to revitalize the Light Body on those days when we feel drained of energy.[17]

The Seer's hermetic remote-healing method

Calle had moved to Fuengirola on the Spanish Costa del Sol. Every morning from 8 to 9am, he treated people from all over the world over the phone. After a short conversation in which the clients explained their problems and where they were located, Calle centred his inner gaze, abandoned any intellectual consideration or judgement, left his body and "travelled" via the ether to the client while his body stayed in his chair with closed eyes and relaxed breathing. He didn't need any information about the client's surroundings or circumstances, it was his/her Light Body that was his target of consideration. The Light Body is the electric/etheric field that surrounds every human being at a distance of about 10 centimetres (4 inches) from the physical body and without which physical existence would be impossible. Calle met the client on the etheric plane, where he quickly checked their condition by scanning their Light Body. Immediately, he was able to locate the problem in the physical body – it was always where the Light particles in the Light Body were weakest. Once he had come to a diagnosis, he began the healing process. He revitalized the weak Light particles with a ray of

[17] See Chapter 18: Practice.

coloured consciousness, gas-blue followed by golden Light, that streamed out of his third eye like a laser beam, which he projected into the client's Light Body.

In this way, he was able to help the thousands of people who contacted him during his lifetime. In my case, I had experienced being in the client's place and thus felt the change that happened through his presence and intervention. Calle brought to life the thousand-year-old practice as described in the scriptures of Hermes Trismegistus, *Corpus Hermeticum* 11:18–22:

"Bid your soul go into any (land you choose), and it will be there quicker than your bidding; bid it pass on to the ocean, and there again it will be as quickly – not as moving from place to place but as being there; bid it also soar up into the sky, and it will need no wings, but yet nothing can hinder it. ... Cutting a way through all, it will soar up even to the last body; and if you should wish to break through this whole also and to gaze on that which is outside – if indeed there be anything outside the universe – you have the right.

See what great power, what speed you have! And when you can do this, cannot God? In this way, then, understand God as having all things as thoughts in Himself – the universe, Himself, all. Unless therefore you make yourself equal to God, you cannot understand God; for like is understood by like.

Expand yourself to the same extent as the immeasurable Greatness; leap out of all body, and transcend all Time; become Eternity, and you shall perceive God. Realize that to you nothing is impossible; believe yourself immortal and able to grasp all things – every art, every science and the way of life of every living creature. Become higher than all height and lower than all depth; gather in yourself all the feelings of the created (elements), of fire, of water, dry and wet.

(Perceive) that you are everywhere at the same time – on earth, at sea, in heaven; not yet born, in the womb, young, old, just dead, the after-death. Having perceived all these at once – times, places, facts, qualities, quantities – then you can perceive God.

But if you imprison your soul in the body and insult it, saying, 'I know nothing, can do nothing; I fear the sea, I am unable to climb into the sky; I know not who I was, nor do I know who I shall be' – then what have you to do with God? For you can (understand) nothing beautiful and good if you love the body and are bad.

For the utmost evil is the ignorance of God, while to be able to know and will and hope is a Straight Path leading through the Good and easy for you to tread; it will meet you everywhere and will everywhere be seen – both where and when you do not look for it, waking, sleeping, sailing, walking, by night, by day, speaking, keeping silence. For there is nothing which is not an image of (That)."

In the *Gospel of John,* Yeshua emphasizes this attitude by quoting the *Book of Psalms*:

"Is it not written in your law, 'I have said to you, you are gods'?"

It is important to understand that there is no heresy or megalomania involved in this statement of Yeshua. It is clear that the words "You are gods" are in direct contradiction to the following Christian dogma, which is still preached in many churches: Yeshua is the only begotten son of God. If that would be so, how can we be children of God too, and even gods ourselves, as Yeshua is saying in the above quote?

The Aramaic *yeeheedaya* has wrongly been translated *as the only begotten* but actually means *the first born*. Through this very different understanding of the Aramaic term, we learn that Yeshua is our older brother, who incarnated here many lifetimes ago to show us the way to our Enlightened Being within. So, when he is quoting Psalm 82, it should be seen as an expression of our divine heritage as children of God, holding the essence of the creative power of Divine Consciousness within ourselves.

Yeshua says in the *Gospel of John* (14:12):

"He who understands my work will follow my example, yes, he will even be able to do greater works than I!"

If we understand, believe and accept what is written in *Genesis* 1:27 – that man is created in the image of God – shouldn't we also take the consequence and actively acknowledge and live with the awareness of the God Consciousness we have been given? This is what Calle took responsibility for in his own life and work, and it was through the access of God Consciousness that he helped thousands of suffering people around the world.

The essence of my training was first and foremost based on a recognition of all my preconceived ideas about what it means to be a spiritual person. By then I had read and studied so much that I had created an idealized but unrealistic image of masters and avatars that was rather rigid. Where the intellect cannot go any further, right there, the spiritual world begins. We arrive at a gate. When we walk through it, we will leave the realm of the intellect, of intelligence and psychology, behind us and enter into the realm of spirit, where intuition and love reign. When we stand at the threshold of the gate and have done the necessary shadow work, realizing the habits, prejudices and blind spots that have ruled us in so many of life's important relationships, and managed to transform the shadows, we step over the threshold, free from the ego's demands for control and comfort, applause and attention. And even then, we must be prepared to always stay in contact and surrender to the still inner voice of ours that always radiates peace and solutions of clarity and harmony. In the beginning, it is very easy to forget and come back through the gate to the loud and all-dominating voice of our personality that creates emotional drama, uncertainties and confusion.

The whole process can be compared to learning to ride a bike. There is no book that can teach you this. Someone might show you how they do it. You can see and trust that it will work. But at some point, you have to get on the bike yourself, try to keep your balance and steer safely through a sea of obstacles, all of which must be recognized and transformed. It requires you to be sober in every way, able to look yourself in the eye and feel your heart. Then you can read the traffic rules. And that's what most spiritual books are, travel guides that share the experiences and the frequencies of other travellers. These can be inspiring, but at the end of the day it's our own inner answers, visions and experiences that matter for our journey.

Inner visions

My life has always been characterized by visions, carried by the inner certainty that has been with me since childhood. I realize now that many of these visions are addressing contents or issues we are facing in the world right now. But even though they are visions that relate to the collective level, they obviously also have affected me on a personal level. In contrast to my research, which has often led me to find quite diverse or even opposing interpretations of spiritual concepts or terms, these visions have been totally clear and straightforward. The same goes for information I receive when watching or reading the news. For example, I read an article about the declining quality of drinking water and immediately had a vision that showed the impact of agriculture on the aquatic environment. I have watched a news programme about a war somewhere and hear the reasons for it, while in an inner vision I immediately see and understand the real background. It is shocking that the majority of the justifications we are given by various decision-makers and relayed by the news media are very rarely in line with the truth. Therefore, it is often difficult for me to understand how we can continue to trust politicians, political institutions and the conventional news media.

Nobody in their right mind shops in a store that has been caught cheating its customers time and time again. This does not seem to apply to the pharmaceutical industry, for example, where some companies do not shy away from commissioning the writing and publication of reports on their drugs and other medical products, falsifying research results or bribing doctors, health authorities and politicians. Government officials are allowed to buy shares in companies that they are supposed to regulate. Several of the largest pharmaceutical companies have repeatedly paid fines for their offences without this leading to changes in business practices. In addition, we live in an age where anyone who dares to ask critical questions is immediately dubbed a conspiracy theorist, a term that has become a label, indicating that such kind of a person's information or criticism cannot be trusted.

In the New Testament, we can read how Yeshua enters the temple courtyard, overturns the tables of the money changers and merchants and chases them out, shouting "You have turned my Father's house into a den of thieves!"

Where does that leave us? What are we doing? "Get behind me, satan, thou art an offence unto me: for thou savourest not the things that be of God, but those that be of men!" Yeshua says to Simon Peter when he doesn't understand what Yeshua is trying to tell him. The term "satan" comes from the Aramaic root sata meaning to mislead, miss the mark, slip, slide, deviate from one's course. Satan is everything that is connected to the duality of the human ego/personality, the part of us that, for example, can easily do charity work, but always wants an appropriate "payment" in return for its effort.

Right now, in our time, there are large private foundations with industrial economic interests that have turned charity into big business so blatantly that it seems highly unlikely that only a few people have noticed the deception. These are foundations that have lobbied their way into the heart of the WHO, the decision-making bodies of the EU and UN, and the health authorities of many countries. The whole Covid-19 affair is one of the biggest frauds in recent history and is a good example of how disastrous it can be when we humans override our inner judgement. The yoke is not yet lifted and will keep burdening humanity until it is addressed and those responsible are held accountable. This process cannot be about punishment or even revenge, but about clarity and avoiding repetition, so we can move on from old structures and experience a change in our societies that is based on integrity. Citizens were seduced by lies or half-truths. As a collective, we have experienced what fear can do to us if it is allowed to run wild.

I am aware that the above will not go down well with many, but it's a risk I have to take. I was one of the many people blamed by my country's Prime Minister for driving the contagion because we had not been vaccinated for Covid-19. Instead, I took elevated doses of vitamin D, vitamin C and zinc and recorded only one sick day during the two years of hysteria. When the first news of massive deaths hit the public through the media, it was clear to me that something was not right. On TV, it was the vacant stares of politicians and representatives of the country's health authorities using the very same sentences in their statements all over the world and the incoherent explanations that seemed to change from day to day, while at the same time it was the duplicate repetition of the fear-mongering by world media, that did the trick. I had to take responsibility myself.

We live in an age where we have been brought up to believe that there is conventional medicine for every ailment, which we usually take without question and without regard for possible side effects. Side effects that often give rise to new diseases and disorders without us realizing the connection.

Again and again, it must be emphasized that when we cut ourself off from our true existence and the soul's purpose of our present incarnation, we are a "kingdom out of sync with itself – and it cannot stand". And this applies to nations, governments, federal agencies, industries, media and individuals. We are standing on the threshold of chaos or balance. And it is we who, by getting up from our screens and engaging with the decisions of our politicians, must make the choice. In this way, the ability to see through any lie has always played a part in my perception of the world and its current state, even though all too often I have not received concrete solutions or have not acted on every impulse I felt. For me, it has always been a question of finding the balance between my emotional reactions and my inner guidance.

When I met Calle, it was very much about learning to let go of the control fixation, while my visions often required controlled action. And I realize that this is a paradox we are all subject to and perhaps struggle with. There is one certainty though that keeps lifting me out of any struggle, once I remember it. Whatever action our individual visions may lead us to do, the Golden Rule of Life should never be broken by us: do not do to others what you would not want done to yourself.

Rebirth in the Church of the Sacred Heart

In the six months before I was to meet Calle, a crucial episode occurred that would have a radical impact on my future. It was a spring day in 1999, just after I had got up from my sickbed. I was in Copenhagen to attend a board meeting of the composers' and songwriters' association DJBFA (now AUTHOR) and was staying at Hotel Guldsmeden at Vesterbrogade 66. That morning I woke up with a deep longing for God. In the lobby, the concierge told me that around the corner there was a Catholic church that held morning masses and I would be able to attend if I hurried.

I ran as fast as I could.

As I entered Jesu' Hjerte Kirke (The Heart of Jesus' Church), I saw a Vietnamese woman take a wafer from the plate set out for those who wanted to participate in the communion and place it in a bowl so the priest would have the right amount of wafers for the communion near the end of the service. I passed by as I did not want to take part, found a seat in the last row and quietly slipped into my prayer and meditation.

Shortly after, the priest came in and began the service. We were about 30 to 40 participants that morning, and I remember getting tense and annoyed by the sound of the priest's scratchy voice triggered by a loose connection in the speaker system. I don't know how long this went on for, but suddenly, like a bolt from out of the blue, I felt a hand resting with full force on my right shoulder. As if to wake me up. I turned round, startled. An indefinable, ethereal figure hung pulsating in the air right behind me. Then he was suddenly there. Clear and distinct. His eyes looking directly into mine as he silently reached out his pierced heart toward me. YESHUA! It all happened so fast, but there was no doubt.

And then I broke down. I sobbed loudly as tears ran down my cheeks. I tried to control myself, but it was impossible. It was like a flood breaking through a dyke that has been hermetically sealed for far too long. I sat hunched over, struggling to control myself with my face hidden in my hands, trying in vain to avoid disturbing the service.

The next thing I recall is that I was standing in the line of people to receive communion. I remember thinking *I haven't taken a wafer from the plate*. At that very moment, I had eye contact with the priest, and everything turned into slow motion. He took a wafer and lifted it up, splitting it in two, as if to show me that now there was one for me too.

When I reached the altar, I stood before him, aghast

and existentially naked, and it seemed to me that he was my witness. He saw me that morning. I left the church, transfigured. I almost floated away. Everything seemed so clear and precise.

For a long time afterwards, I could feel the sensation of Yeshua's hand on my right shoulder. I had been set free at the same time as I had been given an obligation. I had made a covenant about a task that had to do with the dissemination of my studies. Through the sacrament, I had agreed and said YES.

It was after this incident that I began to see small luminous particles or crystals around people. The crystals pulsating around a person who was an old soul had a deep pink colour. In pregnant women, the crystals intensified around the heart and stomach. The crystals by the stomach were always small and brightly coloured, while the heart crystals had greenish or pinkish hues. There were also differences in the formations of the crystals. Quite often, they had abandoned their original harmonious symmetry. Only in a few auras were they in the most beautiful order.

It was also during this period that my Aramaic studies reached a new depth. For months, I focused on the Aramaic understanding that "Light" means "consciousness". As an example, take this scripture from the *Gospel of Mark* (4:21–25) and the *Gospel of Luke* (8:16–18), which is in my opinion one of the most important statements in the New Testament:

"You do not put a light under a bushel, nor do you hide it under the bed. No, you put it on a lamp stand so that everyone can see by it. There is nothing hidden that shall not be revealed, there is nothing secret that shall not be exposed. I beg you, pay attention and take in my words! With the measure that you measure out, you shall be measured out, yea, if you understand this, you shall even be given more in addition than all that was originally made available to you. For he who has understood this/achieved this awareness, to him shall be given more; but he who has not understood this/achieved this awareness, he shall lose even the little he has."

Please, take a moment and read it again. *You do not put a light under a bushel, nor do you hide it under the bed.* Haven't we all put the Light of our true consciousness under the bushel of our personality, and hid it away under our beliefs, norms, insecurities and fears? The "hidden" to be revealed is all that we have been given, all layers of our consciousness, our original condition, all our qualities and our purpose when we were created as souls before the beginning of time.

At some point, our true Being will want to be expressed and lived by us anyway. *There is nothing hidden that shall not be revealed.* So why not focus with all our heart and mind and express it right now? All the ego's agendas will also be revealed and transformed. Either they will be acknowledged by us and transformed in that way (At-One-ment), or they will be exposed through our contact with others (trauma and drama). Either way, one day the ways of our personalities will change. Why not now?

Every veil must fall for us to realize who we truly are. Nowhere else in the New Testament does Yeshua urge us to listen with such an intensity as in the quote. The present reality we find ourselves in is always directly proportional to the way we manage or take care of our gifts and qualities. When we act in accordance with our true purpose and the Law of Light, when we are synchronized and balanced with Divine Truth, then we shall never lack anything, because we are on the frequency of *Rukha d'Koodsha* (the Holy Spirit) that permeates and connects everything. When we turn our backs on our destiny and allow ourselves to be consumed by the material world and our insatiable need for physical comfort and attention-seeking entertainment, we give up even the little contact with God Consciousness we may possess.

This is why the rebirth Yeshua speaks of in the *Gospel of John* is so important to remember. We are given an opportunity, that may first appear as an uncomfortable interruption to a life that – despite the signs that are often given beforehand – continues unabated because we believe that we are unable to change course.

Each one of us, in this current incarnation, even in this very moment, is the essence of all our previous and future incarnations. It is not important who we have been in previous lives or will be in upcoming ones, but what experiences we have had and can bring with us into this incarnation. The moment we need these experiences in this lifetime, they emerge from an opened access to the Akashic consciousness and we may wonder where the knowledge has come from.

Everything we have done in our life and in previous or upcoming incarnations, regardless of the planes or universes on which they took place, leaves a mark in the etheric memory, the Book of Life, while they are themselves the result of past actions and intentions.

When we want to surrender to intuition, we must first be able to set aside even the smallest physical or personal need for a while. This is the stage in our journey when the master calls us to the edge and asks us to step out into nothingness. You have to give up control, which is almost always fear-based. The moment you understand Yeshua's words from the *Gospel of Mark*, "To him who has faith, all things are possible!" and realize what these words imply, you understand that instead of falling into the abyss, you are carried up by a force that cancels the law of gravity and awakens the ethereal powers that are inherent in all humanity.

Faith, *haimanootha* in Aramaic, does not mean blind faith but a trust and integrity that rests on a heart-based, intuitive insight that we have perceived from our original state of consciousness and that has already been proven by our own experience to be true and trustworthy for our personality. It's a certainty that is able to discern and see clearly, even if it cannot always be put into words. Once we live under the ruling presence of *haimanootha,* everything in our life, our fellowship with other humans and all other beings, is thus completely synchronized, side by side, interactively connected with each other in perfect harmony with God Consciousness.

Yeshua's healing method

It was also during this period that I learned about Yeshua's healing method. I focused on collecting and integrating everything I ever read on Yeshua. My daily meditations led to a flood of downloads that I felt urged to write down immediately. His healing method was based solely on his continuous contact with the Holy Spirit. Like the Essenes, he knew and taught that the Holy Spirit, *Rukha d'Koodsha,* is the key to the Kingdom of Heaven, *Malkoota d'Shmeya.*

Rukha means spirit; breath; wind; air; electricity; emanation of life force; magnetic power, while *d'Koodsha* means holy; the way it was meant to be; being in accordance with universal laws; IT IS; the sacred point to which everything seeks; a sacred circle unfolding with power and warmth.

From time immemorial, it has been known by the wisdom keepers on this planet that breathing is the key to the transpersonal state, *Malkoota d'Shmeya.* Remembering this knowledge and dedicating oneself to stay in conscious connection with one's breathing is one of the paths that lead to freedom. Breathing costs nothing and is always at hand regardless of what situation we find ourselves in.

The very sound of the Aramaic *Rukha d'Koodsha* triggers the piercing and activating frequency of pure Life force that includes the vibrational fields of Grace, Wholeness and Harmony. It was this frequency Yeshua was talking about when he stated that only slander/rejection of the Holy Spirit is "unforgivable", as it would eternally separate us from the true reality of Divine Consciousness (*Gospel of Mark* 3:28–29). In other words, *Rukha d'Koodsha* is an awakening force without which we will not be able to rise above a merely materialistic way of living. It is a force that must be noticed, honoured and connected to with the frequency of unconditional love if humanity is to have any chance of transforming itself by activating its spiritual qualities. The way our relationship with the Holy Spirit is will determine how our relationships with any other part of creation will be. *Rukha d'Koodsha* cancels out any error, as well as any consequence of error, and enables us to live in accordance with our true nature and in the Heavenly flow of existence.

Yeshua lived in a field of high frequency that was sustained through his knowledge of, and union with, the *Heavenly Father*, the source of the I AM or Divine Consciousness. Virtually everything he said and did was metaphysical and mystical in nature. He healed by the laying on of hands and by uttering words of healing power. He spoke in allegories and metaphors and used methods that have been known among shamans, healers and prophets for as long as there have been people on Earth.

Yeshua was at his time referred to as a *circle drawer*. When he healed, he cast a circle – that is, he established a force field around himself and infused it with the power of his conscious breath, *Rukha d'Koodsha*. In doing so, Yeshua activated his inner Kingdom of Heaven, *Malkoota d'Shmeya*, which now streamed out from his centre and formed a sacred space. Once the circle was established, he invited the sick person to enter it so that he or she could share in the surplus of energy/consciousness that Yeshua had built up through his breath and trust in/awareness of *Rukha d'Koodsha*.

The transpersonal psychology within the Aramaic language contains the ancient certainty and wisdom of the heart that knows the process of breathing is like a sacred bridge: we abide at one end of the breath and God at the other. In this way, we converse with God Consciousness every time we breathe and are aware of the life-sustaining power of the breath as well as the transformative power of every spoken word or sound.

When two people kissed each other (kiss = *napshak*), it was understood among the Therapeutae over 2,000 years ago that they "shared one breath", connecting with each other through the Holy Spirit or holy breath. And when a person leaves this world through their last sigh, it is said in an Aramaic expression that this person crosses the "bridge of breath" *(gishra d'nshamta)* for the last time to take part in the divine life on the other side of the veil between the worlds.

When Yeshua healed the blind and deaf-mute, he invited the sufferer into his circle. He took some earth, spat on it and put it on the blind man's eyes while whispering the word of power *Ephatah* in the deaf man's ears (*Gospel of Mark* 7:32–35 and John 9:6–7). Yeshua always concluded his healings with the Aramaic blessing *Ikhal* followed by the words *Shlama Alakhoom*, peace be with you. Rise up and let your SHM shine freely. *Ikhal* means: Be blessed and protected for all eternity.

PURIFICATION, BRIDAL CHAMBER AND GUARDIAN ANGELS

Once, a smile revealed all it had healed

Calle Montségur's work with me started with him collecting stones at the foot of Montségur mountain and putting them in my backpack, which I carried up to a ledge near the top, where I was instructed to put down the heavy burden and take out the stones, one by one. Each stone symbolized a relationship in my life that I had to face and transform before I was ready to say goodbye to it by throwing it over the edge of the mountain. And no stone was left unturned, as the saying goes.

We always worked in the off-season, with no other people on the mountain. The weather was challenging, cold, rainy and windy, making both ascent and descent a potentially dangerous endeavour that required my full presence. After three, sometimes four such trips in one day, I was totally exhausted. Yet it felt that a thorough inner cleansing was taking place and a lot of old stuff within me was being transformed. I was so tired that I wasn't able to think even one thought. Instead, a clearer inner vision developed. In the evening, we prepared simple meals, reflected on the day's work and went to bed early. The table was cleared, as we say in Denmark. The next morning, I heard his voice through the wall of his room: "I hereby dedicate myself to the universe!"

He later challenged me to do this too. Because, as he said, it's all about what intentions drive us. Why do we do what we do? What is it that we want to achieve? I struggled, feeling awkward in the face of his brisk attitude, while he kept asking me to repeat the dedication again and again, until he finally was satisfied with my expression: "Now you mean it!" he beamed with joy. *I hereby dedicate myself to the universe.*

Later, I fully understood the power and relevance of this daily dedication, because I had experienced for myself what a difference it made in my life. Why don't you try it too? There is no doubt in me that you will experience a different form of clarity, vitality and belonging when you state out loud who you are and what you have come here to accomplish. Be aware of the power of every single word you speak. To me, it feels like a prayer and at some point, after continuously practising it, you become one with that prayer. The sound of the words and their meaning sets the ether in motion and awakens the frequencies within you and around you that are needed to realize your intentions. It's so simple that at first one thinks it cannot be real. But it is. Anyone can practise it. However, one important thing to keep in mind, is that our intentions must be in alignment with the purpose we set for ourselves before we entered the incarnation. Here, the previously mentioned Law of Light comes into play. The Law of Light, that is part of the God Consciousness and acts as a mirror of destiny in which we can always see if we are on the right path. Does the reflection correspond to the soul's original purpose? If not, we now have the opportunity to correct our attitude. But it is clear that this requires our total presence. And presence is often forgotten and left in the outskirts of our awareness, like a background music that we know is there but never really listen to because we are too easily absorbed by the dramas of everyday life, which are mostly nothing more than expressions of ego strategies and tiresome games that ultimately only create noise and frustration.

The note I wrote as a child and hid behind the wallpaper above my bed was a declaration of intent. It was an expression of an unconscious desire on my part to be able to become the version of myself that was in line with my overall purpose in life. And this is how most of us, as children or young people, may have sown seeds whose fruits we won't be noticing before much later in life. It may be the encounter with the story of Joan of Arc that inspires us, as it did inspire me, to such an extent that we are drawn to the same motives, the same passion, truthfulness, unshakable faith in the messages she received and trust in the guiding voices she was able to perceive that characterized Joan.

I have witnessed many life stories that grew out of an unconscious childhood seed-dedication, such as a woman who unconditionally devoted herself to fighting for vulnerable children. She told me that as a child she had been completely captivated by Joan of Arc and that this captivation had guided her for most of her life. Through her fervour and determination, she was able to bring about improvements in the social system that others had struggled in vain to implement for years.

Throughout the nine years of working with Calle, a whole new vision developed within me, triggered by the different practices he introduced me to. It was a new way of approaching the openness within that before had caused so much pain. Now it was cleared of my personal obstacles. I had become so spiritually robust that I was now able to handle all the impressions and information that I had struggled with as a child. And I couldn't help but think of Yeshua's words: "When you become like children again, you will enter the Kingdom." If only we understood that these words refer to the state of openness and presence that we naturally find ourselves in as children and that Yeshua believes should be cherished. And exactly this state of openness, dedication and trust, that Calle exercised when he was working with clients or practising his confirmative mantras, became a huge inspiration to me. Had this knowledge been part of what adults passed on to us children, I would have been able to embrace and share the revelations that characterized my childhood, instead of hiding them away in a hidden closet of my heart.

During the seven years I spent writing *The Ө Manuscript,* I experienced that everything I needed was given to me immediately, sometimes even before I realized that need. Food was delivered, money for bills arrived in surreal ways, any relevant information flowed freely and came to me randomly at all times, day or night. It would appear as downloads, sometimes even as a literal dictation. Before I took it further and let it form the basis of my writing, I compared everything I had written with the results of the studies I had done in the previous years. For example, the research on the relationship between Mary Magdalene (the Exalted) and Yeshua the Nazarene (the Chosen).

The Bridal Chamber

In the late 70s I acquired a copy of *The Nag Hammadi Library in English,* the English translation of the scriptures and gospels found in Nag Hammadi in 1945, a discovery that was one of the many numerous synchronicities in world history. There seemed to be a direct link between the first nuclear test in the Alamos Desert in New Mexico and the discovery of the Nag Hammadi scriptures. The atomic bomb was the culmination of science's many years of search for God in matter. The first splitting of the atom took place in 1932 at the University of Cambridge in England. But instead of God, they found humanity's darkest shadow. The first nuclear device was tested in July 1945 in a desert in New Mexico. The code name for the operation was "Trinity". A few months after the test, another, much quieter and life-giving "bomb" went off in another desert: the discovery of a collection of Christian and Gnostic texts, later named *The Nag Hammadi Library*. Thirteen leather-bound papyrus codices in a sealed jar that had been buried in Egypt 2,000 years ago, suddenly emerged from the sand as a divine answer, a balancing act to the development of the atom bomb, to the so far most devastating implementation of human destructiveness. The cosmic message was clear: Yes, there *is* a God! Just take a look and see what you'll find!

Among the scriptures, the *Gospel of Thomas* stood out as the most important text in understanding the Law of Light. But the *Gospel of Phillip* has also proved to expand our perception of early Christianity, as well as our awareness about the relationship between Mariam and Yeshua.

The *Gospel of Thomas* testifies that its authors had great metaphysical and psychological insight:

"If those who guide you say to you, 'Behold, the Kingdom of Heaven is in the sky,' then the birds of the air will precede you. If they say, 'The Kingdom of Heaven is in the sea,' then the fish will come before you. But the Kingdom of Heaven is within you and everywhere around you. If you know yourself, then you will be understood (seen as you really are) and you will know that you are children of God. But if you do not know yourselves, you dwell in poverty and you are poverty." (*Gospel of Thomas* 3)

"When you make the two one, when you make the inside like the outside, and the outside like the inside, and the above like the below, and when you make the male and female into a single being, so that the male is not male nor the female female; and when you can see with new eyes, and can see a new hand in the hand,

and a new foot in the foot, when you have seen your true Image, then you shall enter the Kingdom." (*Gospel of Thomas* 22)

"He that hath ears, let him hear! There is Light within a Light-man, and he enlightens the whole world. If he does not shine, there is darkness." (*Gospel of Thomas* 24)

"He who knows everything, but lacks himself, lacks everything." (*Gospel of Thomas* 67)

"If you bring forth that which is in you, that which you bring forth will save you. If you do not bring forth that which is in you, that which you do not bring forth will destroy you." (*Gospel of Thomas* 70)

And in the *Gospel of Philip*:

"Truth did not come into the world naked, but it came in types and images. The world will not receive truth in any other way. There is a rebirth and an image of rebirth. It is certainly necessary to be born again through the image. Which one? Resurrection. The image must rise again through the image. The bridal chamber and the image must enter through the image into the truth: this is the restoration."

"The apostles before us called Him, 'Yeshua the Nazarene, the Messiah.' Yeshua first, Messiah last, and Nazarene in the centre. Messiah means 'The Anointed One' and 'He who is set aside for a higher purpose.' In Aramaic, Yeshua means 'freedom' and Nazara means 'truth'. Therefore, the Nazarene is the truth, the liberator and the chosen one."

"The Nazarene is the visualization of the invisible."

"A woman's children resemble the man she loves. When it is her husband, they resemble the husband. When it is her lover, they resemble the lover."

"Even the worldly embrace is a mystery; and still more mysterious is the embrace that embodies the hidden union. It is not merely the reality of the flesh, for there is silence in this embrace. It does not arise from a random impulse or from desire, it is the result of will. It is not of darkness, but of Light."

"Faith is to receive and love is to give. No one can receive without faith and no one can give without love. We believe and are therefore able to receive; we give to experience love. He who gives without love experiences nothing of interest."

"Wisdom *(sophia)*, who is considered immaculate, is the mother of Angels. The beloved *(koinos)* of the Son is Mary Magdalene. He loved her more than the other disciples and often kissed her on the mouth."

And here is an important statement made by Yeshua from the Aramaic *Gospel of the Nazarenes*, also known as the *Gospel of the Holy Twelve* (66:7–9):

"Again I say to you: I and my bride *(kalta)* are one, just as Mariam Magdalene, whom I chose and dedicated to myself as an example, is one with me."

In this statement Yeshua says: I have come to know the feminine principle *(kalta)* in me, and I have seen this principle mirrored in a woman, Mariam Magdalene, whom I have therefore chosen as an example to me because we are one.

It is clear – after reading all the gospels and writings that deal with Mariam and Yeshua's relationship – that they were a couple and that the wedding in Canaan was most likely their wedding. Additionally, the fact that Yeshua and Mariam "kissed often" (see quote above) indicates that they were both initiated into one of the mystery traditions of the time. In Yeshua's case, the teaching and subsequent initiation (baptism) undoubtedly took place with the Essenes, while Mariam, I am certain, was initiated by the Therapeutae at Lake Mareoti outside Alexandria in Egypt. It is known that the initiates kissed each other on the mouth to recognize, acknowledge and revere each other. Just remember the Judas kiss. Through the above understanding, we now know that Judas must also have been an initiate.

As mentioned before, the kiss had an overarching meaning. The Aramaic *napshak* means *to share the same breath*, and that two people become one with each other through the God Conscious breath. This makes it a sacred act that expresses complete presence and total devotion. As you can read in the quote from the *Gospel of Philip* above, a woman's children resemble the man she loves. "The lover" here is an expression for *Rukha d'koodsha,* the Holy Spirit, which a couple knew manifested when they consciously entered the Bridal Chamber to become one there. For when two people unite in God Conscious love, even though they may not create a child, they always create a third entity, a gestalt or image in the ether. As the author of the *Gospel of Phillip* writes, although even the physical embrace can be rightly called "a mystery", there is a "mysterious embrace", in which every touch and kiss is made conscious and becomes thus an expression of the devotion and fervour of God Consciousness that sets the highest frequencies vibrating. It is when the masculine and feminine principles disappear into each other and become one, where the personality (ego) is transformed and the two in the One can move mountains. This embrace is not the result of desire but of will. A conscious choice and dedication. *It is not of darkness, but of Light.* In the bridal chamber, as well as in all other spaces in our lives, EVERYTHING that one does can be transformed into a blessing and sacred act.

If we, the so-called evolved, educated and civilized people, understood the implications of this process, intimate relationships between two people would take on a whole new meaning. For example, two people who truly love each other could meditate on the prayer below before their time together in the Bridal Chamber. Writing the prayer down as a declaration of intent and hanging it above the bridal bed would be a blessing in itself.

The Bridal Chamber Blessing

In this sacred space of love, truth and trust,
we hereby bless our love for each other.
We open ourselves to the union
of our souls and bodies.
We dedicate our presence on Earth to the revelation
of harmony and healing.
May every kiss and touch, every delight and joy
lead to the manifestation of truth, love and compassion
for all Beings everywhere.
May clarity and vision be revealed and received
through the embrace of the Divine Feminine
within the shelter and strength of the Divine Masculine.

Guardian Angels

Every human being, from the moment they are born into the world, is accompanied by a so-called Guardian Angel. A Guardian Angel is an ethereal Being of Light who resides in the etheric field of Consciousness, usually invisible to the incarnate. The Angel helps their human to make the best out of the choices they make.

The concept of free will is a widely discussed topic in spirituality. It is a popular expression to say: *We were given* the freedom to choose. By whom or by what? By God. If we take this revelation out of the familiar context of a Father/ Mother figure and remember that we are talking about an all-harmonious Consciousness here, we will understand that it was not given to us, it *IS a given*, an inherent part of our being, it IS a part of us. We have the freedom of unlimited access to a neutral, all-harmonious creative force, under any condition at all times. And we create what our mind and heart are radiating. No words can disguise or hide our true state of being.

We are constantly manifesting our choices. If we are not present, the process of creation happens without our conscious awareness. In this case, our unconscious beliefs, thoughts and emotions weave the frequencies of our day-to-day experiences without us even recognizing it. So yes, we have the freedom to choose and do what we feel is right, but very often our choices are not in line with the deeper understanding of our inherent divine essence that would allow us to see our own responsibility, our overall purpose or the timing of our desire to realize a choice. This leads to a number of perceived "set-backs" or "detours". And it is in those times of challenge in which we can most clearly feel that our Angel is closest to us. For example, if you experience resistance to an initiative you have taken, be it a business opportunity or a crucial life choice you have made, it may be your Angel helping you in such a way that your endeavours do not succeed – because if they did, it would perhaps lead to greater misfortunes than the resistance you feel. Maybe the time is not ripe for the manifestation, maybe you are not. Only later will you understand the reason behind the stagnation or "failure", and perhaps you will remember to thank your Angel for the intervention and thus avert disaster. Remember also the Aramaic understanding of good (ripe) and evil (unripe or rotten) as explained earlier.

I have always felt the presence of my Guardian Angel as far back as I can remember. At one point I asked the Angel for their name. The answer came to me in a dream one night, a few years after Daisy had returned from Israel: *my name is Ishatar!* The next morning, I wrote the following to my Angel:

"'Look inside yourself,' you said, even though you knew I was already in there and only wanted to break out. 'Look down to the bottom of the soul,' you said, even though you knew I was already down there and too small to want anything but to fly up. Oh Ishatar, how we ran. Across the endless grass of childhood. You were always with me, walking with me in the rain and sitting by my bed when I was sick. Where did we run Ishatar, where did you go? If only I knew everything now that I knew then I would never have believed all those lies: out of sight, out of mind. Then I would have known that you were with me in the prison in Jaffa to show me that that prison was but a caricature of the far darker prison I afterwards brought with me everywhere. Oh Ishatar, had I not confused freedom with lies, had I not hidden my nakedness behind my foolish, pathetic mask. I wouldn't have stood here so haughtily between all my loose words, never felt the need to live up to all the rules by which they decide whether one is small or great. Then I wouldn't have celebrated all the falsehoods and would never have killed anything but known that every goodbye is just the beginning of something new."

While Ishatar was my Guardian Angel, I sensed that she also represented the feminine aspect of me. It was a thought I dwelled on for a long time – was it Ishatar who had embodied herself as the girl in the blue swimsuit by the Varde River to make herself known? And was she perhaps also the woman that the main character in my book *Zoé* was looking for?

In 2006, an incident occurred that lifted another veil. I had just finished a busy season of workshops and was travelling home by car from the Pyrenees. I had set off at 02:00 in the morning and at quarter to eleven the following morning, I had reached the vicinity of Dijon in northern France when I was jolted out of a momentary doze after hitting the crash barrier at 140 kilometres (87 miles) per hour. I remember turning the steering wheel sharply to the right at that moment to further avoid the barrier, only for the car to roll sideways across the carriageway as I flew at breakneck speed through a white tunnel, my body left to its own struggle for survival in the car, which was now also doing head-on somersaults before twisting through a fence and sliding two metres (6.5 feet) down into a field.

When I came back to my body, it was through the crown in the centre of my head. There was a small pop, like the sound of pulling a cork out of a bottle. Fifty metres away was the car, totally crushed and with one headlight on in the drizzle. The first thing I thought was that I was dead. The silence was unreal yet comforting. Then I looked up. Ten metres in front of me stood a young woman, bright and beaming. Around her neck she wore an equilateral cross. She encouragingly said:

"If you can survive this, you can survive anything."

Only then did I notice the worried German man squatting next to me. He told me that I had got out of the car myself and laid down just outside the car door. He had helped me move further away for fear of the car exploding. It felt strange, even for me in the state I was in, that the young woman and the man did not speak to each other at all. The last words I heard when the rescue team came to pick me up, were uttered by the young woman, who encouragingly said:

"Don't worry, everything is taken care of."

The last image I saw through the back window of the emergency vehicle was her waving to me with a big smile. At the hospital, they realized that apart from the muscles in my body, which were as sore as if they had been subjected to ten rounds with Mike Tyson, I had not suffered the slightest injury. There was no doubt in my mind that it was my Guardian Angel, Ishatar, who had manifested herself for me and helped me through the process.

We all have an Angel by our side. That's why it's so important to be present, to be able to receive the signals these Beings of Light are constantly trying to send us. Ishatar is my muse, my inspiration and my intuition. It's only when I'm lost in worldly matters or in my personal ills and errors that I momentarily forget her presence. When we alternately under- or overplay our cards or give control to ego strategies, we lose ourselves. Through meditative work and heightened awareness, I sense her close by. Always near and always there to guide me.

11

THE WORLD OF QUESTIONS AND THE WORLD OF ANSWERS

"I don't know where to go!"
cries the arrow to the bow

What is the cause of thousands of people having the same, apparently supernatural experience, such as the apparitions of the Virgin Mary over the Coptic Church in Zeitun, a suburb of Cairo, Egypt? During a period of approximately three years, beginning on 2 April 1968, Mary could be observed two or three times a week, appearing above the church as a floating light, sometimes as a figure with clearly visible facial features and at other times even surrounded by twelve luminous doves. She was filmed, photographed, drawn and painted, standing still or floating around. Countless people who had witnessed the apparition experienced a miracle of healing and were officially declared healed and healthy.

What happened when a Catholic woman, Myrna from Soufanieh, a suburb of Damascus, suddenly experienced that oil started to flow out of her hands while praying in the circle of her family for her sick sister-in-law? How is it possible, that, after Myrna had put her hands on the woman's back, she was healed? What is the reason that, some days later, a plastic icon of the Virgin Mary and the child Jesus that had been purchased in Bulgaria, begins to emit oil with healing properties? What is going on when, immediately after Easter, Myrna shows the signs of stigmata for the first time, bleeding from wounds on her forehead, side, hands and feet, just like Yeshua, a condition that recurs every time Easter falls on the same date for the three Christian churches? Just as Padre Pio experienced in the 1930s in his monastery in Italy, where he bled the wounds of Christ until his death in 1968.

How does it happen that Yeshua appears to people out of the blue, as I experienced in the Church of Jesus' Sacred Heart in Stenosgade in Copenhagen, or that my Guardian Angel manifested as a physical being after my car accident outside Dijon in France? Yes, history is full of such revelations by the thousands, from Fatima in Spain to Lourdes in France and Medjogorje in Bosnia. If we understand that everything created is a projection emanating from the all-encompassing God Consciousness and that all creation is abiding within it, we have to accept that every soul is an individualized expression of this God Consciousness – otherwise it could not be all-encompassing.

Consequently, we too have the ability to create through projection. And that's what we do, mostly unconsciously, around the clock, throughout our lives. What separates the unconscious from the aligned conscious is that the latter triggers harmonious projections into the ether, individually and collectively. When Yeshua says in the New Testament: "Knock and it shall be opened," he invites us to focus our consciousness on the goal we have set for ourselves, for example, to solve a vital problem. This can be done through a spiritually grounded practice. Once we have found the right password, the corresponding gateway will open.

To succeed, we need to adopt an attitude through which we are able to let go of the ego and intellect's need for attention and control for a moment and open to the ever-present reality of pure creational vibration. Know thy Self. The key words are: Heartfelt and self-transformational surrender.

With such an attitude, we will eventually, through patient practice, become one with our goal.

The day I had my encounter with Yeshua, I was totally raw and open. I was filled with an unknown longing. Something needed to be released that somehow had made me want to take part in a church service. I even ran to the Church of Jesus' Sacred Heart in Stenosgade. Following that intuitive urge, I was sending a signal that was beyond any kind of pragmatic reason. It was my heart that ran. I wanted nothing, not even to participate in the Eucharist, but sat in the last row and surrendered to the moment. In the clarity that had appeared afterwards and the visions of luminous crystals I began to see around people,[18] I realized that this was a communication with a higher layer of consciousness or a similar frequency in the ether and that it was through my silent cry for help that the gate opened, and the archetypal image of Yeshua appeared to me. There was a synchronicity between my heartfelt desire and the collective field that contains all known archetypes. Remember the statement from the *Gospel of Phillip*:

"Truth did not come into the world naked; it came as archetypes and images for the world to receive it."

And the whole process I went through, giving in to the calling from my soul, running to the church, shows how we can unconsciously experience breaking through the veil that separates the World of Questions from the World of Answers. Only when I started working with Calle Montségur a few months after this experience, did I realize how it is possible to consciously make contact with the World of Answers. This is achieved, as I said earlier, through a purposeful disregard

---

[18] Dorje Jinpa describes in his book *SENSA, The Lost Language of the Ancient Mysteries,* how every soul has an etheric signature consisting of archetypal geometric shapes that can be read in the ether by anyone if we open ourselves to them.

for any form of control. You could say that it's a form of re-programming that overrides the learned and established ways of our intellect, which always thinks it can figure things out and has things under control, but which falls completely short here and thus ends up in pretence and powerlessness.

As Bishop Eugraph Kovalevsky says in connection with the contemplative state he himself works with through the Orthodox Heart Prayer, and which also applies to my approach of abandoning the limitations of the intellect and the obstacles it presents when we want to connect with the higher intuitive layers of consciousness:

"From the moment you start to 'think' – in the literal sense of the word – you are not intelligent."

We are confronted with the limitations of language, as language is never able to reach beyond the speaker's or the listener's own imagination. The word "love" is not love. We can use the word, but it only expresses the idea of love, not love itself. On the other side of the veil, in the World of Answers where the intellect has no access, you become *one* with love. You express the meaning of the word because you have *become* all that the term and concept contains without ever thinking "love". Calle always emphasized that it was inappropriate to limit yourself with phrases like: "I can't do that!", because this kind of belief would be a blockade you would have to deal with later. He repeatedly told me that a lifetime of such negative, but unfortunately normal, mantras would ultimately cause illness and cut us off from any contact with the World of Answers. When Yeshua used the Aramaic commandment *Ephatah,* it was precisely to dissolve limiting attitudes such as "I will never get well," or "Sickness is my destiny," which only keep the sick person suffering.

Never give up – always *give it up!* Up to the God Consciousness in you. To the higher vibrating harmonic frequency that is our essence, instead of the disharmonic frequencies of any form of suffering. That is why Yeshua's statement that we must become like children again is so important. Of course, such an attitude does not mean that we should adopt an infantile attitude, but that we should seek and express the unreserved openness of a child. As adults, we should then be able to reflect on and distinguish the experiences we have had in the open, non-judgemental and free certainty of a child, that is available to anyone with the necessary patience and discipline.

The Jewish mystic and philosophy professor Simone Weil often spoke of man's transcendental abilities that unfold when we allow God's grace to penetrate our very centre, and from there illuminate our very being, making us able to walk on water without violating any law of nature. She also stressed how, when we turn away from God, we simply surrender ourselves to the law of gravity. Then, if we think that we can decide and choose, we reduce ourselves to being only things or stones that fall.

Asking for clarity and confirmation, I once sat down with the question what the difference was between my encounter with my Guardian Angel and my encounter with Yeshua. The answer came immediately: my meeting with Yeshua had been, like most apparitions, an archetypal image that appeared on the veil between the physical and ethereal reality, while my Guardian Angel was an ethereal Being of Light, a gestalt that is part of the individual's Light Body and is therefore linked to his or her personal etheric imagery.

In my case, the Being that suddenly manifested as a young woman – and seemed completely unimpressed by the car accident I had just survived – took on the image of my ideal inner, feminine aspect that I carry and honour in me. Angels are etheric Beings with the ability to manifest themselves physically anytime. To my knowledge, the Guardian Angel of a man will manifest as a representation of his ideal woman, both physically and spiritually. For a woman, her Guardian Angel will manifest as a representation of her ideal man.

The car accident happened during a period when I had been regularly communicating with this Being of Light, my Guardian Angel Ishatar, in the etheric opening between wakefulness and sleep. There I saw her sitting at one end of a cream-coloured sofa, while she invited me to sit next to her at the other end. From her I received advice and information, which I subsequently wrote down and used in the last book of *The Θ Manuscript*. She became a link to the collective records I was meant to access in the Book of Life and the World of Answers. If we are able to examine these records more closely, we will receive insight into the true proceedings of the world historical events through the ages. This is exactly what the seer Edgar Cayce, like the prophets Isaiah, Daniel and St John, warrior Saint Joan of Arc, the stigmata Catherine Emmerich and clairvoyant and spiritual researcher Madame Blavatsky and many more were able to do.

Most visual artists, composers and writers, in their best moments, receive inspiration of various kinds from the World of Answers. However, most of them are unaware of this relationship, which all too often means that some feel called upon to process and "improve" the information and images they receive. Trusting the received as a completed and self-sustained creation can be challenging. Yet to me, exactly in this acknowledgement lies the nature and essence of art, which begs the question: does the true meaning of the term "art" include any form of trickery or any performance or displays of something bizarre, like the freak shows of yesteryear?

I experienced this feeling myself, of being compelled to change what I had intuitively received before, while living on the island of Samsø. One winter's day I was invited to visit a sacred site on the nearby islet of Hjortholm in Stauns Fjord, a small waterhole named "Frejas Øje" (The Eye of Freya). Hjortholm is a nature reserve, and it is forbidden to go ashore as a regular visitor, so I was very excited and grateful. Stauns Fjord was used by Viking chieftains who came from all over the north to meet here on "The Island of

Gatherings" to divide the land and kingdom between them, agree on new raids and settle feuds and disputes. The chiefs brought their shamans with them, who consulted the runes when big decisions had to be made and the gods consulted. It is said of the "Eye of Freya" that the waterhole never dries up or freezes. Through her Eye, the goddess Freya looks up into the sky and into the soul of those who spend time on the banks of the waterhole. That's why I wanted to visit the place.

Søren, a shepherd I had come to know, was going out to the islet to check on the sheep, but because of the frozen fjord and the danger of falling into hidden wakes in the ice, he had to bring a companion for safety. We each carried a 3-metre-long (10-foot) pole and were connected by a rope tied around our waists.

The myth turned out to be true, as the "Eye of Freya" was the only one of the four waterholes on the island that had not frozen over this winter. While Søren continued his journey to the smaller islets, I stayed at the "Eye" where, in the hour it took before Søren returned, I wrote down the 211 four-line verses that today make up my book *Freja's Prophecy*.

When I got home, I put them in a drawer, and it wasn't until spring had arrived that I found them again, thinking that here was very good but quite raw material for creating a collection of poems about Samsø. It was six months later at the reception of the book on the day of publication while I was making an introductory speech that I realized what a huge mistake I had made, so I asked the attendees to return the books they had just bought. Afterwards I visited all bookshops they already had been distributed to, and then spent a couple of years buying up and destroying the copies that had escaped the bookshops as well as all copies I found in antiquarian bookshops.

I was searching for a way to balance my feeling of failure, my lack of presence that I was judging as a folly and a nuisance – which confronted me with the concept of penance. Although I was aware that there is no reason to focus on self-humiliation or mortification once we understand the essence of God Consciousness, as it will only keep us out of the Holy moment of Now, I still felt that I had to devote myself to right a wrong before I could feel at peace with myself again. So, I printed a new edition, without all my additional poetic inventions, at my friend from Daisy, Poul Erik Veigaard's printing workshop, *Fingerprint*, bound 100 copies by hand and gave them the title *The Forgotten Language*.

But it wasn't until I found the original handwritten manuscript a few years later, that I was able to clean the book of the last overlooked leftovers of my additions and let Lindhardt & Ringhof publish the Danish edition. The German edition *Die vergessene Sprache: Frejas Weissagung* that followed had been straight translated from the original text.

This was a great lesson for me, and it was a huge relief to be able to remove all my personal quibbles so that today the book appears in its purest form, exactly as it was written at Hjortholm.

When we consciously begin to establish contact with the World of Answers, we realize that no matter what is received, the information and images are always filtered through the transmitter – our personality. If the personality takes up too much space and therewith cuts the connection to the inspirational flow of information or frequencies, it can, as the above example shows, interfere with the purpose of the creation, distort the immediate communication and turn the eternal into a passing fad. This is why the work of clearing our awareness of mental and emotional noise is so important, because it will eventually transform indifferent, personality-based art that is inspired by the experience of duality, into soul- and spirit-based, prophetic, healing and insightful works that are inspired by the principle of harmony and that will open the transmitter and receiver up to higher frequencies of consciousness.

12

HORIZONS OF THE PAST

Be blessed, in movement and rest

It took me many years to learn to live with and understand my innate intuitive sensitivity, which in my early childhood often left me lonely and alienated. Later, when I realized through my studies that there were other people who faced the same challenges, I arrived in the world. My fascination with the Essenes of the Dead Sea, awakened by Daisy's tour to Israel in 1969, led to visions of a past life as an Essene 2,000 years ago. It was Calle who helped me understand this belonging. He called me "The Scribe" right from the start of our time together, and when I asked him why, he promptly replied: "You were a scribe to the Essenes, where you copied some of the treatises that today make up the Dead Sea Scrolls. You copied the Book of Enoch and the Book of Psalms, among others. That was your occupation."

He once pointed out to me that it was not always necessary to know who you had been in previous lives, but that it is the essence of the experiences you have had in other incarnations that is important. If it is appropriate to know any details about a specific incarnation, you will of course receive the relevant information about it.

One night, within the first weeks I was with Calle in the south of France, I had a dream. I was standing on the top of Mount Carmel in Israel, before humans on Earth were created. It was at the very spot on which the Prophet Elijah aeons later would establish the School of Prophets. I was in a spiritual form, still not manifested in the physical, yet present, looking out over the most beautiful landscape imaginable. The sensation was of a dawning morning, the sun rising over the horizon, its golden rays playing in the morning mist. Out of the mist steps an old rabbi dressed in white. He holds out a white book to me with the words: "The time has come for you to get to know this one." I immediately realized that this rabbi was an early incarnation of Yeshua as the Essene Teacher of Righteousness.

Later, I read in an old scripture – today known as the *Damascus Document* – that he was the one who (approximately 100 to 200 years before his incarnation as Yeshua) led a big group of followers from Israel into the Syrian desert west of Damascus, where he established the first Essene camp outside of the School of Prophets on Mount Carmel. The scribes who worked under him in the Syrian camp documented some of his teachings in the *Damascus Document*. "The True Teacher", as he was called, died in this Syrian exile. In the wake of his passing, his followers returned to Israel where they built the university at Qumran by the Dead Sea in the spirit of their beloved Teacher. The dream activated a stream of visions of my former life with the Essenes. I am convinced that this dream and the following information were triggered by Calle's access to my former life as an Essene scribe.

The Essenes and quantum physics

The Essenes, or Sons and Daughters of Light, mastered the art of metaphor which, together with their Chariot of Fire practice, enabled them to contact the World of Answers and access the Book of Life. A continuous practice of the Chariot of Fire prayer makes it possible for the practitioner to see a reflection of his/her current state of being in the mirror of the Law of Light. Our conscious way of breathing, while being present in the Chariot of Fire practice, is the bridge between the physical and the celestial realms. It is by *becoming* this practice with all its inherent frequencies, that we leave the World of Questions and enter the World of Answers.

The teachings of the Essenes were all-encompassing. The theories of today's physicists about nonlocality in particular are merely a rediscovery of what the Essenes already knew so many years ago, based on experiences gained through profound practice. To them, all creation is an interactively connected field of energy. When most people today use expressions like: "What a strange coincidence!" or "There is more between heaven and earth" after having experienced unexplainable phenomena, for the Essenes, no occurrence in their lives was random. They perceived reality as an unfolding of vibrations, manifested as connected synchronicities.

"My Father's kingdom has many mansions," said Yeshua, the long-awaited Messiah and reincarnation of the Essene Teacher of Righteousness. There are other worlds, other realities and other planes of consciousness on which humans can incarnate. These other realities are parallel universes that can be contacted outside of time and space.

The Essenes realized that humans are a projection of God Consciousness. A projection that has the ability to project too, as the projecting Consciousness and the projected consciousness are One. In our creational process of our own projections, we can always project "back to God", meaning staying with the awareness of our soul to finally *become* our purpose in everyday life.

They knew that everything, at some point, returns to its origin. What exists somewhere else also exists right here. What does not exist here, doesn't exist anywhere. It would therefore be meaningless for the Essenes to imagine that by sending a physical spacecraft into so-called outer space, they would find something that did not already exist here. For them, it was through the journey inward and toward eternity that knowledge of other realities was received.

Essene Mystery School was a sacred education that offered a millennia-old spiritual science. Their interactive system of instruction, learning and exploration was based on the understanding that intellectual knowledge can never stand alone, as it needs to be guided by the wisdom of the heart. There, soul and spirit are residing in communion. Any information, any belief, any theory, even those that we have taken for granted and stored as *facts* in the layers of our consciousness can only be recognized and validated as *Truth* through our own metaphysical study and experiential practices that must always go hand in hand.

My past with the Essenes

The following information arrived over a period of about one year at the beginning of my apprenticeship with Calle. He helped me to keep asking the right questions and to meditate on them until I got answers. Some information came in bits and pieces, while others came in longer downloads. I discussed everything with him and whenever I was in doubt of anything concerning the visions, he helped me clarify and decipher them. Throughout my life and work I have been led in many different ways toward my Essene roots. And now I know why. On a personal level I had to free myself from the religious rigidness that has been part of many of my former incarnations. On a soul-purpose level it was, and still is, the task to convey the true teachings of the Essenes and anchor their vision of unconditional love.

Two thousand years ago, Israel was divided into small independent territories. The Jews were called Judeans and mainly lived in the region of Judea, which had Jerusalem as its central city. The Samaritans and the Galileans were not reckoned by the Judeans to be Jews, even when many of them followed the Jewish customs, religious convictions and practices. Compared to the more sophisticated citizens of

Judea, they were seen as being rural and simple people. Many Essenes were Samaritans and Galileans, which might have played an important role in how they were perceived by the priesthood in Jerusalem. This of course raises the question of whether Yeshua and his family were Jews or Gentiles?

My name was Asaph. I was born to Persian parents in Jerusalem but was given into the care of the Essenes when my father died and my mother was unable to care for me. As a young man, I was taken to the university at the Gate of Hope (now called Qumran) on the shores of the Salty Sea, called Asphaltis by the Romans (now called the Dead Sea). There I began my training as a scholarly scribe. The sole purpose of the Essenes was to prepare the way for the long-awaited Messiah, called by the brothers and sisters the Teacher of Righteousness or The True Teacher. All our writings were aimed at this common cause.

My education consisted of copying the massive library of prophetic literature that filled the shelves in the hall where I and the other scribes were working and included an understanding of scripture and its hidden meanings. I also learned to employ various codes and ciphers. It is important to consider that not all accounts in the *Pentateuch* (*Torah*) and in some of the *Prophets* are based on historical facts. They must be understood symbolically and metaphorically. The people, kings and prophets mentioned were real historical figures, but in the scriptures, they express different aspects of human nature, physicality, psyche and spirit.

But beyond these insights there are even further contents and meanings in the scriptures. The Essene elders who led the university were aware of prophecies hidden in multi-dimensional codes behind the ordinary text. Today, through advanced computer programs, the first layers of the hidden codes have been uncovered. One day we will realize the extent of the hidden knowledge – seven different layers will be found in many of the texts discovered in the caves around Qumran as well as in many of the scriptures of the Old

Testament. These are prophecies of future events and insights into our human heritage that will allow us to fully realize the God Consciousness we were given when we were created as souls before the beginning of time.

Rabbi Yacov Rambsel revealed different codes concerning Yeshua that have been placed into *Isaiah,* Chapters 52–54. In 53:10 he found the following words behind the ordinary text:

"Yeshua shmi" – "Yeshua is my name".

In the same chapter, all the names of Yeshua's disciples are mentioned: Shimon Petros, Ya'acov ben Zabedai, Yochanan, And'drai, Pilipos, Toma, Mattiyahu, Ya'acov ben Chalipi, Shimon Hakanai, Taddai Lebbaeus, Mattiyah, and last but not least, the three Marias who always followed Yeshua, Mary (Yeshua's mother), Miriam Cleophas (Yeshua's sister) and Mariam Magdal (Yeshua's beloved partner). The content of the text behind which the hidden information was found, tells of the passion of Christ.

My teachers were able to perceive, read and manifest codes of knowledge in a scripture. They had so many years of practice as Chariot of Fire travellers that they, while writing down the first layer of the stories, automatically experienced a direct connection to the World of Answers and the Book of Life, which manifested as holographic downloads within the texts.

My education also included the vast knowledge of the 22 letters of the Aramaic alphabet. Each letter expresses a specific creational frequency. When accessed, one receives knowledge about each of their meanings and the workings of the archetypes to which they are connected. We meditated on all letters over and over, until they became part of our very being. I so very deeply enjoyed this way of learning.

We were taught about the human physique, psyche and spirit, about the stars in the sky and their harmony with humanity, about herbs, plants, stones, the power of crystals, the power of song, healing and prophetic sense. All lessons of knowledge were held in between lessons of spiritual practices, purification ceremonies, baptismal practices, prayer, our individual morning and evening meditations and the Chariot of Fire practice *B'Shm Adonai*:

> "B'Shm Adonai
> Mi ya meini Michael
> U mi smoli Gabriel
> U mi lifanai Uriel
> U mi achrorai Rafael
> Ve al roshi Shekinah El
> Ve ba levi Meshiach."

> "In the Image (and Frequency) of God Consciousness
> (I call upon)
> Michael on my right side
> Gabriel on my left side
> Uriel in front of me
> Rafael behind me
> Shekinah above me
> And in my heart the Messiah."

Michael: The Knight of God. The One who takes responsibility for the creative powers of God Consciousness within him. The understanding, acceptance and embodiment of all Divine Qualities.

Gabriel: The Voice of God. Our higher Intuition. The dedication to perception beyond our personality.

Uriel: The Fire of God. The Purifier. The Cosmic Pedagogue. The frequency that brings clarity through purification. Removes obstacles and shows us the right path.

Rafael: The Healing of God. The Restoration of Truth. Brings unconscious patterns to Light and removes disharmony.

Shekinah: The Presence of God. The Spirit of the Divine Feminine. Mother/Essence of all that is manifested.

147

Messiah: The Anointed One. The Restorer. The Redeemer. The One who experienced rebirth. The integrated frequency of being on Earth without any earthly chains.

This practice was repeated for hours until the practitioner became one with it and lapsed into a trance-like state, from which we left the physical body and, under the protection of the frequencies the Archangels represented, ascended to higher planes of consciousness.

Enoch has described this state in the *Book of Enoch* where, with the help of the Archangels Michael, Gabriel, Uriel and Raphael, he is lifted up to the highest realm of creation.

There he sees the firstborn (*yeeheedaya*) soul to incarnate on Earth, "The Son of Man" (the first incarnation of Yeshua as Adam, the first human on the Earth), and witnesses how the spiritual DNA of this elder brother of ours was being bestowed with the qualities of "The Ancient of Days" (God's Divine Will/Kether of the Kabbalistic Tree of Life). "The Lord of Spirits" is an English translation of the Hebrew/Aramaic *YHWH Tzva'ot* (God).

"And I asked the angel who was with me and who showed me all things hidden concerning the Son of Man, who he was and why he went with the Ancient of Days? And he answered me: 'This is the Son of Man, who possesses righteousness, who rests in righteousness and who reveals all the precious things that are hidden, because the Lord of Spirits has chosen him, because his kind takes precedence in righteousness with the Lord of Spirits forever.'" (1 *Enoch* 46:2–3)

"And in that place I saw the fountain of righteousness, which was unquenchable, and around it were other fountains of wisdom, and all who thirsted drank from it, and were filled with wisdom, and their dwelling was with the righteous and the elect. And in that hour the Son of

Man was spoken of before the Lord of Spirits, and his name mentioned before the Ancient of Days. Yes, before the sun and the signs were created, before the stars and the heavens came into being, his name was mentioned in the presence of the Lord of Spirits. He shall be the rod wherewith the righteous shall lean, that they fall not; and his shall be a light unto the Gentiles, and a hope to the despairing hearts. All who shall inhabit the Earth shall follow him and his example and shall praise with song and blessing all that is made by the Lord of Spirits for ever and ever." (1 *Enoch* 48:1–6)

In the *Gospel of Thomas*, logion 50, the following words of Yeshua are quoted in an instruction manual for the Chariot of Fire traveller:

"Yeshua said:
'If they say to you, "Where do you come from?"
say to them, "We come from the Light, the place where the Light came into being by its own accord and established itself and became manifest through their image."
If they say to you, "Is that you?"
say, "We are Its children, and we are the elect of the Living Father."
If they ask you, "What is the sign of the Living Father in you?"
say to them, 'It is movement and rest.'"

Who are the "they"' that Yeshua is referring to here? They are the threshold guardians at certain interdimensional gates who are there to ensure that the traveller is aware that he/she is now crossing the threshold to a new and higher level of consciousness. Their task and purpose is to protect the physical, mental and spiritual wellbeing of the traveller. The phrase "movement and rest" refers to an eternal surrender to the rhythm of creation, where the inhalation of a breath is always followed by an exhalation, and we are the ones being breathed and moved by its sacred current. Both, our actions as well as our awareness about our very being, must always be based on an active presence as well as a readiness to rest in God Consciousness.

We were between fifteen and twenty brothers living permanently at the university, but we were regularly visited by brothers from other settlements who were going through different initiations at the university. When a brother completed all the brotherhood's programmes, he received the holy baptism followed by the last initiation called *Forty Days in the Desert*, which meant spending forty days in an unprotected and spiritually open or naked state in the cave known today as Cave 4.

Half of the approximately 5,000 Brothers and Sisters of Light who were in Israel at the time, lived along the shores of the Dead Sea, south of Qumran. The majority of these were settled on the great plateau of Ein Gedi, on which one of Israel's oldest kibbutzim stands today. Just like then, I still love visiting this place, an oasis in the Judean desert.

In the Essene community were many married couples, who lived in houses that served as hostels scattered across the Middle East from Damascus in Syria to Alexandria in Egypt. These couples who ran the hostels provided help and healing in the local area where they were situated, and the hostels functioned as guesthouses for the brothers and sisters who were travelling between Essene settlements.

The teachers and scribes lived in the university grounds, and the three oldest of them were the three wise men, the Magi, who left one day when they interpreted the astrological signs that showed it was time to head west to Bethlehem, where the new incarnation of the Teacher of Righteousness, the anointed high priest and king, would be born.

The rest of us eagerly awaited the return of the three elders so we could get all the details about the returning Messiah. Yeshua was not an orthodox Jew, but a Nazarene. One of his ancestry lines was rooted in the Nazarene tradition, which was part of the Essene brotherhood. *Nazari* means *One who is set aside to serve a higher purpose; the one who knows; the initiated one.* The Nazarenes also originated from the School of Prophets on Mount Carmel, a school founded by the Prophet Elijah and later led by his student Elisha. It is important to remember that these two, hundreds of years later, incarnated as Yochanan the Baptist (Elijah) and Yeshua the Nazarene (Elisha), and that the place in the Jordan River where Yochanan baptized Yeshua was the exact same place where Elijah passed his wisdom and cloak to Elisha before he left the earthly reality in his Chariot of Fire in a state of transfiguration. The account of Elisha's healing work is completely identical to Yeshua's many years later. Elisha performed feeding miracles, he healed the sick and raised the dead, which can be read about in the Old Testament, *Second Book of Kings.*

Yeshua's parents Mary and Yoasaph belonged to the brother and sisterhood of the Essenes. Immediately after the birth, they brought the child to the temple in Jerusalem, where two Essene prophets, the Elders Shimon and Hannah, were waiting to receive the Messiah and perform his circumcision. They had both foreseen the coming of the child and knew that they could not leave their earthly existence until this act had been carried out by them. The incident is described in the *Gospel of Luke* (2:22–38) in the New Testament.

The parents then travelled with Yeshua, accompanied by two Essenes, to the temple of the brother and sisterhood in Heliopolis, Egypt. When the boy was twelve years old, he was brought back to Jerusalem to celebrate what today is known as *bar mitzvah.* At Yeshua's time, many poor families gave their firstborn (*yeeheedaya*) son to be raised as deacons or servants in the Temple of Jerusalem so their families could obtain certain privileges and a social status that made them respected members of the community. The priests and rabbis of the temple knew about Yeshua being revered as the Messiah but refused to even consider him because of his Essene heritage.

It was on this occasion that one of the Brotherhood's highest-ranking teachers, Hillel, wanted to gain the Sadducees' and Pharisees' acceptance of Yeshua as the lawful Messiah long awaited by the prophets. Yeshua was subjected to questions, which he readily answered and the Light that was said to surround him was so bright that the learned priests were completely blinded by it. However, the priests' amazement was quickly replaced by anger when they realized that the boy was far superior to them in understanding the scriptures, and they accused Hillel of blasphemy.

Yeshua's education took place mainly at the University of Mount Carmel. Here he studied under a female teacher named Judith Mare (Judith, the Master). She was an Essene but with a background in the Zarathustra tradition and was an exceptional teacher of the highest calibre. Shortly before Yeshua's decisive journey to Persia, he, along with Master Judith and their entourage of five brothers, stopped at the University of Qumran. It was on that occasion that I saw him for the first time. And there was no doubt in my heart that he was indeed our long-awaited True Teacher and Teacher of Righteousness. Meeting Master Judith also left a deep impression on me. She was the first woman I had contact with at that time, and she radiated such authority, clarity and compassion that the combination of these qualities, united in her, became my ideal of how high a human being is capable of reaching.

Three years later, Yeshua and Master Judith returned to our university, where it became my task to show Yeshua the work of the scribe, the handling of the skins and papyrus, as well as the meditative, patient practice that is fundamental to the work of any scribe when meticulously copying manuscripts. If an error occurred on a scroll, it had either to be discarded, or we cut out the column with the error and replaced it with an added sheet of papyrus with the rewritten passage.

It was on that occasion that I realized that Master Judith had transferred her highest qualities to him. He did not reveal this in words, for he was silence itself, but through his bare and clear presence. There was something unfathomable about his being, an inexplicable charisma that gripped your heart. Together with him, you couldn't help but be deeply moved. After a few weeks, the group travelled on to Heliopolis in Egypt, and when Yeshua was thirty years old, he returned once more to Qumran, where he underwent the final initiations of baptism in the Jordan River and forty days in the cave of the university.

The Essenes knew the importance of water for all life and treated it with the highest respect. Their rituals for the physical purification were embedded in a deep communion with the frequency and wisdom of this element.

Later, when I worked with Calle, he helped me to remember my knowledge of this ancient science. For him, as for the Essenes, the main aspect of working with water was to transform its frequency back to its original, divine state, connecting it to the mother of all water. This practice of transformation can be integrated in any healing methods and applied to all elements, materials as well as to any situations. Calle had developed a technique that involved visualizing gas-blue Light being beamed through the palm of one hand into a glass of water followed by the visualization of beaming a golden Light. When you feel that the water is clear, you bless it by placing your palm over the glass while visualizing the presence of the mother or the source of all water and reciting the word of blessing: *Ikhal – Be blessed and protected.*

The brothers also used prayers and blessings written on small pieces of papyrus that we placed in small containers, called *phylacteries* or *tefillin*, which we wore on the forehead next to the third eye. For it was written: "A sign on your hand and a symbol on your forehead ..."

Yeshua has explained the power we receive when we focus on the third eye (*Matthew* 6:22):

"The Light of the body is in the eye: if thou therefore shalt make thy sight one (see and act through the third eye), thy whole being shall be filled with Light."

I always carried the priestly blessing, which was translated thus:

> May the Heavenly Source of all Being
> bless you and keep you,
> may the power of Grace radiate and vibrate
> through you and give you peace.
> Amen.

When the brothers realized that I had a gift for singing, the *Book of Psalms* became the focal point of my education. Very early on, I understood how invocations are one of the most direct forms of communication with God Consciousness, the Heavenly Source of all Being.

After the initiation at Qumran, Yeshua went directly to Canaan where he married Mariam Magdal, who was also an initiated master. Yeshua's marriage to Mariam and their subsequent mission was not looked upon favourably by all of the brothers, as many did not understand Yeshua's true purpose. I heard that on several occasions Yeshua had to speak in capital letters to these brothers, whom he compared at such times to Pharisees.

Before I left the earth plane in that lifetime, I was able to experience Yeshua and Mariam on one occasion: when she anointed him for the second time. Some years ago, after I had a vision of that memory, I realized that you can't mention Yeshua without also experiencing Mariam. The two are simply one. It was during this initiation that Yeshua said these words:

"For this act alone, Mariam Magdalene shall be remembered forever."

It is therefore strange that we have completely forgotten or deliberately disregarded this testimony to her authority and instead for centuries considered her to be a prostitute. According to the Jewish and Essene precepts, it is not possible for a non-initiate to anoint an initiate. Therefore, of course, she was an initiate too, who even bore the initiatory name *Magdal* (the Exalted One).

The following passage from the Dead Sea Scrolls, fragment 4Q521, puts the Essenes' expectations of Yeshua as Messiah into perspective:

"For heaven and earth will listen to His Messiah, and none will depart from the predictions of the saints. You who seek Him, arm yourselves for His service. Will you not thereby find the Master – you who patiently wait for Him in your hearts? For the Master will come to the pious, and the righteous He will call by name. And His spirit will rest on the humble, and the faithful He will renew with His strength. For He will honour the awakened man on an eternal royal throne, setting the captives free, opening the eyes of the blind and raising the lowly. And I will cling forever to those who hope, and to the luminous reality that has not been before, the Master will realize as He has said, for He will heal the sick, raise the dead, He will preach good to the oppressed, the poor He will feed, the homeless He will lead and the hungry He will enrich."

13

VISION, MEMORY AND EXPERIENCE

Has the heavenly sphere always been here?

"Memory is experience," writes Jack London in his novel *The Star Rover*. In the book London is describing how the life prisoner Darrel Standing – when lying for weeks wearing a straightjacket in a confinement cell – was able to leave his body and "visit" former incarnations that appeared to him during these trials of torture that went on for most of his time in jail. The novel is based on the real story of Jack London's friend Ed Morrell, who told the author about his experiences in San Quentin.

Today's science teaches that a large part of our memories are post-rationalized by our subconscious, to fit into the self-perception we build up throughout our lives as well as to bypass traumatic experiences. There is an interplay between our self-perception and the way we manipulate our memories to maintain the reality we want to uphold. We all know how old stories between friends get better and better as years go by. But how much do we actually remember? Perhaps we can find the most interesting and meaningful aspects of our past experiences in those parts of our memory that we repress or deliberately exclude?

However, the kind of memory this chapter is about is of a different nature and is similar to Ed Morrell's straightjacket experience. It comes to us in ways other than the kind of experience where we try to remember certain events and, as mentioned above, shape them until they fit our self-perception.

The memories that I want to focus on here often show themselves as archetypal symbols. When you begin a spiritual practice in which you can rest and thereby awaken to a faster vibrating frequency, memories will begin to appear in dreams and as momentary influxes of material that are either psychic or spiritual in nature. The psychic information will relate to the current incarnation, while the spiritual information comes from the etheric frequency on which the Book of Life resides. These relate to past or future incarnations. Throughout any and every of our incarnations, we carry the information of each of our lifetime-experiences in our Light Body and we are, consciously or unconsciously, always influenced by their energetic essence in our field.

The moment we enter a conscious spiritual path, our former beliefs about our self will undergo a change, and psychic memories of both a supportive as well as challenging nature will surface. Layer by layer, we are starting to peel away the different identifications of our personality, learning more about who we are and the reason why we incarnated here. At the same time, we receive memories of past or future lifetimes.

Any memory or vision is either appearing because it will help us to deepen our view about our personality or it will trigger a widening of our spiritual understanding. To consciously include both sources of information while staying aware of their difference will help us to find and walk the ancient path to the cosmic gate *Know Thyself*. No matter what we must master, no matter what memories or visions might surface, they will transform through our dedication, as we continue our path toward spiritual understanding – it is the path to freedom.

In my book *The Seer,* I described how Calle felt a very special and close connection to the Roman Emperor Marcus

Aurelius, without claiming to be his reincarnation. One day, when Calle and I were in a large market in Andalusia, Calle suddenly pointed to a stall with old coins and said: "I have a feeling there's something there that belongs to me." When we later visited the stall and opened the folder of coins on display, we realized that it was an ancient coin with Marcus Aurelius' counterfeit in profile on top. And it was certainly not unlike Calle's profile. After that episode, I read Aurelius' masterpiece *Meditations* and must admit that there are so many similarities between the philosophy of life expressed in the book and the one that formed the basis of Calle's being and outlook on life. The combination of Stoic willpower and universal compassion is similar for both the Roman emperor and the Andalusian seer. When asked about the reason for such re-incarnational connections, Calle explained that, in his own case, it could be because he had been associated with the Stoic philosophy in a previous life or could have been in the staff or family of Marcus Aurelius and thus had a close relationship with him. The same, he believed, applies to anyone who feels they have lived through the incarnation of a famous historical figure. Because, as he said, how many Mary Magdalenes, Genghis Khans, Madame Curies or Napoleons could there have been?

Immediately after my sister's death, there were two historical figures in particular that I felt a very strong connection to, although at the time I did not speculate on the reason why. One was the composer Joseph Haydn and his last symphony, 104, also known as the *London Symphony*, and the other was Thomas Edward Lawrence, also known as Lawrence of Arabia. In the shop window of a bookshop in my hometown, a copy of Lawrence's *Seven Pillars of Wisdom* was on display. On the book's cover, Lawrence was photographed wearing Arabian robes. This picture and the book had an electrifying effect on me.

The strange thing was that every time I played the *London Symphony* on the family record player, the image of Lawrence would appear in my mind's eye. He was always dressed in white Arabian robes and always riding through the desert on his camel, usually alone and only a few times with a larger entourage of Arab warriors. This image only became stronger after I saw David Lean's epic and magnificent, yet highly romanticized film *Lawrence of Arabia* in 1963, starring Peter O'Toole as Lawrence.

But it was only after my experience with the University of the Essenes at the Dead Sea during the Israel tour with Daisy in 1969 that I realized that Lawrence in his book describes the purity of the desert as being *Essene*. During his journeys between Medina and Damascus, he passed through the desert around the Dead Sea many times and must have been familiar with the Essenes and their residences at Qumran and Ein Gedi, just as he must have been familiar with the Arab Sufis, both spiritual movements that have had a great influence on my life.

Today, I am continuing to listen almost every day to one or two of Haydn's 104 symphonies, and I have read *The Seven Pillars of Wisdom* countless times, as well as the endless series of Lawrence biographies that have been published over the years.

It was through working with Calle that I began to understand the nature of the memories associated with the Book of Life. "If we believe that revelations from the Akashic records are accompanied by magnificent, heavenly music and that the heavens open as God speaks to us, we must think again," Calle always said. According to him, revelations of a consciousness higher than our present one are always available, if you contact the right frequency. And forming a habit of doing so, he emphasized, should be as natural as managing any other task in our everyday life.

I had just finished the book *The Seer* when Calle shared his way of working with the Book of Life with me. I experienced it as a shift within myself, like a crack in a wall that had previously been impenetrable for me. Through this opening, a wide range of information of an archetypal and metaphorical nature now manifested in my awareness.

After a month of intense work at Montségur in the Pyrenees, which no longer involved me selecting stones as symbols of my personal relationships and life issues, carrying them up the mountain and transforming them with the help of his presence, but of standing in the centre of the castle courtyard performing a kind of ethereal Sufi dance, he suddenly decided it was time to go south to Spain.

The dance consisted of me standing on the Grail spot without moving my physical body, but with my breath turning my Light Body counterclockwise, thus opening my access to the Akashic records, which was necessary for my dissemination work within the upcoming writing. I came to understand that this practice stemmed from the Essenes and their Chariot of Fire practice. It had roots back to the School of Prophets on Mount Carmel where I believe the Prophet Elias was working with this etherical movement of the Light Body. I haven't been able to perceive from where the practice has its origin but tend to believe that it was brought into the world by the Kamal Posh (*Those wearing a blanket*), a group of mystical wayfarers dating back to long before known history. The Kamal Posh were nourishing the wisdom of mysticism and the basics of spiritual science in their hearts, travelling out of the East into the rest of the world, practising nature medicine and healing. I believe that these men and women also practised this ethereal dance in a form that included physical movement, which was later picked up by the Druids, as well as different early Sufi lineages and especially Rumi, in his school of whirling dervishes. In more recent times, Rudolf Steiner revived the ancient science of conscious movement to access the immanent information within the ether as well as its creational power and to neutralize or transform our daily issues by influencing the human Light Body and the ether through Eurythmy.

It was due to the etherical dance at Montségur that I perceived the title of the trilogy *The ☉ Manuscript*, the

O being a circle with a dot in the centre, symbolizing the presence of both the male and female aspects of creation: The Consciousness of the Heavenly Source of All Being. This was even before I had started writing the second book of the trilogy, *The Magdalene*. I was neither aware of the content of the information I was about to receive, nor of the way it would reach me.

Quite perplexed, it was almost a year later when I realized: if you join the first two words of the title together you get *Theo Manuscript*. "Theo" stems from the ancient Greek word *theos* – God. Without my conscious creational input, will or understanding, the title of the trilogy means: *God Manuscript*.

On our way to Calle's home in Fuengirola, we spent a night in the old town of Toledo. This is a city full of secrets. It seems completely buttoned up and you almost feel that the veil that has settled everywhere here is about to burst at the seams, so much is hiding under the surface. Calle headed straight into the centre of the old city. It was here that he uncovered the city's hidden Kabbalistic Tree of Life matrix, which you can read about in *The Magdalene*.

While in Toledo, Calle began to share his memories of one of his and my past lives together. The following is my paraphrased version of Calle's account from that night in Toledo, when he shared the information he had received on that specific incarnation:

"It was here in Toledo that I, as Master Kyot, around the year 1,000, found an ancient manuscript written in Arabic that contained the story of the Grail. I was a hermeticist and alchemist, with a predilection for Christianity. Because of dark forces that wanted to appropriate the Grail manuscript, I had to take another name, Kansbar. And it was as Kansbar that I met you on the coast of Malaga. Your name was Flegetanis, a Jewish troubadour who travelled around conveying your spiritual insights in poetic verses that you sang in marketplaces. Back then, you lived in the Alpujarra Mountains in Andalusia and were a free soul who was said to draw his wisdom from the stars. Now this lifetime has brought us together again. When we work in Fuengirola, we are at the very place in which we met each other for the first time in that past incarnation. The manuscript is still accessible in the Book of Life, and it is your task to manifest and spread the knowledge of those parts of its text, as well as its vibrational downloads, that have to do with the Source and how humans today can find their true origin and true purpose. You are the Scribe, aren't you?"

But it wasn't until I finished my book on Mary Magdalene and began to work on the final book of the trilogy, *The Grail,* that I had a clue where the information about the Magdalene had come from.

Here is the original Prologue from *The Grail*:

"A few years ago, an old Spanish manuscript was handed over to me. The title was *San Gral* and the author was stated to be *Kansbar.* The old Spanish manuscript is about 400 pages long. It is of no literary value. The contents are more or less uninteresting, at least to the untrained eye. If there is anything in it at all of the slightest interest it is to be found between the lines. And the little the zealous reader may find there is only for the few to whom it has any meaning at all.

Reading the dedication of the manuscript you immediately get the feeling that the contents are a matter between the one in the dedication who is handing the manuscript over and the one who is receiving it. In this case *Kansbar* and *Flegetanis.* The manuscript is dated, 'Alhambra, 1001', and the dedication reads as follows:[19]

---

[19] This dedication is also quoted in the Prologue to *The Magdalene.*

'Kansbar is not my real name. But due to the secrets I have been chosen to guard, I have taken this old Persian name. Kansbar the Chosen One. Kansbar the Wise. Kansbar the Seer. Kansbar the Protector of the Grail. I am getting old.

For many years I have been searching for the one who is to take over this duty after me – but in vain. Only now do I remember the day I met Flegetanis, an itinerant Moorish singer, in a marketplace in a small town on the coast of Andalusia. This manuscript is for him. This is the story of the Grail.'

At the beginning, I didn't know what to do with the manuscript. Apart from a slight curiosity, I just felt a childish pride that I had been found worthy to guard it. Not until I started reading it, finding that the contents did not live up to the promises of the dedication, did my new-found worthiness evaporate like dew in the morning sun.

For two years, the manuscript stayed untouched in the bookcase in my study collecting dust, until the day the sun sent a pale ray onto it as if it wanted to lead my attention to it once more.

Thus, it was totally without any kind of expectation that I opened the yellowed manuscript again. The moment I took it in my hands it seemed that the light in the room changed. I hesitated and looked up from the empty page.

The empty page? Outside, the sun was pale and low in the sky. Apparently, nothing had changed in the room. Only the book. I turned a page. Not a letter. Not a single word. I turned another one, and yet another, only to see that apparently nothing was written in it. Instead, some neat, almost transparent characters appeared on the paper. The strange symbols and signs seemed to move, and the more I looked at them the more the signs danced in front of my eyes, almost teasingly and diabolically.

I sat for a long time, unfocused and ruminating about the strange thing I had just experienced. When once again I looked at the manuscript, the original text was suddenly there on the pages. I leafed through it and saw that, apparently, the text was intact again. Was all this simply a figment of my imagination?

Then it suddenly dawned on me that, although the contents of the manuscript in itself were insignificant, it nevertheless constituted a protective veil, a kind of key to an otherwise closed world. Not until later did I understand that the manuscript was simply a metaphor, a mirror or a gate to another dimension.

The information that the manuscript communicated was only a pale shadow of a much deeper knowledge. The ordinary text told a local story from Andalusia, mainly about two characters, Kansbar and Flegetanis. The inexplicable signs behind the text, somehow, were the key to this deeper knowledge. However, it was a kind of knowledge which only reveals itself to those who are ready for it. The manuscript, then, was a metaphor for a possibility that is to be found in man himself; an access to the so-called Akasha files in the great, ethereal, universal memory.

I turned a page and started reading."

This text is a clear description of the process I went through while writing *The Magdalene*. I needed to be willing or allowing to see through the seemingly apparent into the essential. But does that mean that Calle and I really were incarnations of Kyot/Kansbar and Flegetanis? My experience about, and explanation to this is as follows: both Kyot and Flegetanis entered the world of archetypes when Eschenbach wrote about them in his great work *Parzival* and it became a classic in esoteric literature. It mirrored and personified qualities that are always to hand, but maybe otherwise are difficult for us to identify with. Therefore, they belong to a collective frequency within the Book of Life. Each of such collective archetypes constitute a field of consciousness that holds certain qualities. Due to W J Stein in his amazing study *The Ninth Century and the Holy Grail,* we can learn that Flegetanis is not a name but a Persian word or title for "a person familiar with the stars". He goes on to explain that "any person with such a title would not be an astronomer[20] who observes the heavens with external means, but one who had imaginations or visions of the heavens. It is possible," he continues, "that by this it is intended to indicate the character of such a person's clairvoyance."

Both Kyot/Kansbar and Flegetanis are representing a certain path, and those who, through their incarnations, have followed the same path as these two, would naturally feel acquainted with them. Time and space belong to the World of Questions while the World of Answers is enfolded in eternity.

What happened one week or 2,000 years ago is always present in the eternal now and can be drawn on in an instant. The reality of such insight can be hard to grasp, and even harder to integrate into one's everyday life. How would we perceive ourselves and others, if we would remember that we are experiencing multidimensional insights and impulses when we are talking to each other? Are we ready to integrate this fundamental truth that will lead us to a new understanding of who we really are?

Shortly after I had returned to Denmark from Toledo, where Calle had told me about his and my former incarnation in Spain, late one night I received a phone call from a woman who introduced herself as Birgitte Wallenberg. She was staying in her house in the village of Bubion in the Alpujarra

---

[20] In Eschenbach's *Parzival,* Flegetanis is described as an Arab astronomer who first read the secret of the Holy Grail in the writings of the stars.

Mountains, had just finished reading *The Seer* and asked if we could arrange a meeting. This came to pass about a month later, when Birgitte visited her sister who lived in Aarhus. It turned out that the two were nieces of the famous Swedish diplomat Raoul Wallenberg, who helped more than 100,000 Jews in Hungary to escape from the Nazis during the last year of World War II. We met several times and had close contact. Birgitte invited me to use one of her houses in Bubion, the town's old school, La Escuela, where I wrote a large part of *The Magdalene*. I introduced Birgitte to Calle and they spent some time together exploring the Alpujarra mountains.

In Bubion, there was an unreal silence. The city was white. Everything was painted white. The streets were empty, and the sun was burning hot. It was as if my personality and my loneliness completely dissolved in all this blinding whiteness. I finally understood how my connection to the Book of Life worked. I started to see clearly. It was here in this very place where Flegetanis had once lived 1,000 years ago. It was here. Just like then, this town is still a residence for Sufis. It was here in the blazing white heat that I experienced that I was being purified or emptied of any intellectual input. Instead, I started to pick up strange symbols with my inner eye. The symbols seemed to be some kind of alphabet, but they didn't make any sense to me. At first, I thought that they were Nestorian Aramaic letters but found that it wasn't so. In the beginning, this of course was frustrating, but I felt that there was a hidden meaning behind these symbols and that I had to contemplate each of them one by one. I visualized each one of them and stayed with them as long as I was able to until they began to vibrate, but still I received no clarity, no solution to what they meant. Then I simply started to ask for an answer when I prayed and meditated before I went to sleep. And it was after such a session that I woke up the next morning with a clarity and openness that I hadn't felt before. Then the information on Mariam the Magdalene and Yeshua started to flow. When a chapter was written I compared the information with my studies of Mariam the Magdalene in the Nag Hammadi scriptures and the New Testament that I had started 14 years before. The joy I experienced, when I felt that both of the streams of information, the intuitive and the intellect, were matching in many instances, was indescribable. In this way, my time in Bubion also symbolized a major breakthrough and shift in my way of working. I had found a key to the World of Answers. Birgitte has since left this world, but I am forever grateful to her for calling me that night, as if she knew that there was a man in Aarhus who needed a push.

When I think of how everything seems to be connected, I cannot help smiling, thinking of the days when I met Robert Hauschildt, who travelled with Daisy to Israel in 1969, and how he enthusiastically introduced me to the Spanish classical music of De Falla, Rodrigo, Mompou and a huge selection of flamenco music. Or when, in 1987, I travelled to Granada with a photographer for a week, to shoot photos in the Alhambra for a record cover, without knowing how I was connected to this place. To me it is just another proof that nothing is coincidental, that everything is synchronized and connected. And that many of our visions and creations are based on memories of past experiences.

"The heathen, Flegetanis, could read in the heavens high how the stars roll on their courses, how they circle the silent sky, and the time when their wandering endeth – and the life and the lot of men he read in the stars, and strange secrets he saw, and he spake again low, with bated breath and fearful, of the things that is called the Grail, in a cluster of stars was it written, the name, nor their lore shall fail. And he quoth thus, 'A host of Angels this marvel to earth once bore, but too pure for earth's sin and sorrow the heaven they sought once more, and the sons of baptized men, hold it, and guard it with

humble heart, and the best of mankind shall those
knights be who have in such service part.'"
(Wolfram von Eschenbach, *Parzival*)

This is our calling too. The baptism mentioned in the above
verse is a metaphor for the rebirth Yeshua is talking about.
A rebirth we all have to go through in our present incarnation.
We need to wake up to this understanding, our highest
calling, to take responsibility for the spiritual aspects of our
life and be the embodiment of God Consciousness we were
meant to be. When we take the first step, aiming to live our
lives like the wise men and women who have incarnated
here over and over again to inspire us and show us how to
walk this Earth with a heavenly attitude,[21] all our questions
will be answered immediately, all our needs taken care of.
We too will join them in their wisdom and become who we
truly are: peaceful and creative, caring, compassionate and
joyful residents of this Earth. We are the keepers of the Grail.

---

[21] "A heavenly attitude is theirs; those, whose Love is without condition.
They will, therefore, receive unconditional Love." (*Gospel of Matthew*,
Chapter 5:7)

14

CORRIDORS OF SPACE AND TIME

Can this moment last?
Oh, friends of future and past ...

Any kind of disease can be read in the human Light Body. This is how Calle was able to make his diagnoses, even if the client was on the other side of the world. As described before, Calle "travelled" via the higher and faster frequencies of the ether to the client, performed the necessary examinations and started to transfer pure life energy to those parts of the client's Light Body that needed healing.

In the later years of his practice, he began to work with the upper layers of the ether, where collective information, for example about historical incidences and personalities, is stored. He received new information about the basic elements, which also included an attribution to either masculine or feminine principles, astrological and psychological connections, and he even discovered new elements not yet known to science. This work resulted in a protocol that he worked on right up until his death.

If he had even the slightest personal antipathy or prejudiced and judgemental thoughts about a person or subject he wanted to reach, the ether immediately closed to him. Again and again, we need to live by and embody Yeshua's words that we must become like children to be able to enter the Kingdom of Heaven. A kingdom that, he reminds us, has many layers and realities. This is the knowledge we need to recall if we want to understand the ether and how we can work with it. Calle often said that the universe (the ether) needs us.

Everything so-called negative that we project is the consequence of a decision of ours to leave our identification with the all-harmonious reality. Those projections not only keep us and our immediate surroundings stagnated in the created field of low-vibrational thought forms but will also imprint into the collective ether.

This is why it is important that we understand that absolutely anything and everything we do, say, think and feel plays an important part in the shift of consciousness that humanity is experiencing right now. From a sad or unkind thought to a raised voice to an act of violence, and everything in between. The frequencies of any action we take, any sound we utter, any emotion we express are released into the ether – so it is our responsibility to avoid taking part in the personality dramas that are so prevalent in a world where so much selfishness prevails. Instead, we need to project positive thoughts and desires. If the practice of sharing and receiving unconditional love feels too distant to reach for us, we can start with connecting to others in goodwill. The practice of blessing (see Chapter 18) is also a support for us, if we feel bound in emotional or mental turmoil.

As mentioned, some layers of the ether can act as a canvas on which archetypal images can be evoked, just as scenes from the past can be replayed in the form of a hologram. Through connecting with certain ethereal frequencies, remote viewing and distant healing is possible, and the deceased can appear to our inner sight on some etheric frequencies.

While working with Calle in Spain, we spent a lot of time practising the skill of synchronizing the different levels of our Light Bodies. When we started to work with these levels, it was impossible for me to differentiate between them. As we went on, day by day, I was filled with a liberating feeling of being whole and connected within as well as toward everything around me, and in this case especially to Calle. It was for me the highest degree of joy I had ever experienced. I felt embraced and at the same time felt the urge to embrace everyone and everything. This covered the way to silently perceive and transfer information between us. Through visualization and thought-transfer exercises, we eventually achieved a precise exchange. We would sit with closed eyes opposite each other and he would silently send geometric figures, squares, triangles, circles, etcetera, to me to pick up. Later it would be thoughtforms and ideas. I would do the same toward him. In between we would always connect, practising the *Mirror of the Soul*, sitting gazing into each other's eyes for at least half an hour and sometimes much longer. We continued in this way, until we had aligned our Light Bodies and had established a clear communication on the same frequency. Afterwards I felt how he was able to project or open certain scenarios from our past lives stored in the Book of Life. I also felt that we became much closer to each other.

As emphasized so many times, to succeed in such exercises we must focus on being fully present and be willing to let go of any control, expectation, former references, beliefs, emotions, the will to influence or achieve and let the higher, immediate intuition prevail – which is precisely the natural vibrational field of a child.

When connecting with another person or a layer of the ether, we quickly realize how a myriad of thoughts are clamouring for our attention. For a long time, we have to practise the ability to let our thoughts pass without giving them attention and allow ourselves to take that step into the unknown. Have faith, be patient, pray and the doors will open.

The following passage is taken from my book *The Seer*:

"One day, as the Seer and I walked along the coastal promenade of Fuengirola, we continued past the last hotels and construction sites with half-built apartment blocks, into the poor part of the city, which resembled a suburb. Laundry hung on strings across the streets. A couple of prostitutes stood on a street corner offering their services. Dogs roamed freely and, behind the houses, cockroaches the size of large mice darted in and out between the piles of rubbish. The sweet smell of rat poison mingled with the unmistakable stench of an overloaded sewage system. The houses groaned with eurodisco and fandango. The sunlight was broken by a forest of TV aerials and satellite dishes, making the shadows flicker and dance flamenco in the narrow streets. We had walked for a long time without saying anything. I had the feeling of walking beside myself – further and further into an unreal state.

A dark man crossed the street and disappeared into a small bar. I could hear Arabic music. The atmosphere of repressed life in this labyrinthine neighbourhood somehow corresponded to a shadowy maze in my memory. 'This is the place in your memory that you keep returning to without understanding or making the connection.' I didn't understand what he was talking about.

'What does that mean?'

We stepped out into an old square filled with rickety tables and stalls. The sun was baking. I squinted my eyes to see better. For a moment I thought we were surrounded by people dressed in strange clothes, women in veils and oriental robes, men in cloaks and turbans. The Seer walked into the crowd of people. I followed him. He stopped in the square. 'Feel this place,' he said.

The sun was directly above us. Out of the corner of my eye, I saw the man from before coming out of the Arab bar. The Seer looked right through me. The black galaxies were spinning through the universe. His voice was clear and distinct. Yet it was as if he was speaking from another time.

'We have stood here before. You and I.'

The sentence echoed down the endless corridors of memory. *We have stood here before, you and I – we have stood here before!* Something made me turn my face in the direction of the bar. The sun's rays reflected off something shiny and blinded me. I could just make out a dark figure standing outside.

'I've waited a long time for this moment.' The voice ricocheted off the corridor walls. *This moment – this moment – this moment – this moment – this moment!* At first, I doubted. But then I realized it was true. The dark man was watching us. For this split second I looked into a burning desert of stars and loneliness. Then into ... It was impossible. It could not be. He slowly started to move in our direction. I was about to signal him when the Seer spotted him and grabbed my arm. Everything stood still. Like a held breath. Like a drop caught in the fall before it disappears into the sea. Then the man turned and started running back toward the bar. He was about to knock over a stall of jewellery before he disappeared through the door from which he had come a moment ago. A young gypsy woman shouted after him. I wanted to say something, but the words stuck in my throat. Then I lost sight of her. The Seer stood calmly watching me. It all happened so fast. Around us, life went on."

This experience is an example of an opening of an ethereal memory imprint: the present reality suddenly changes and for a moment we gain access to another life. Both Calle and I saw the square shifting into a different time, we both saw the market stalls, the people in oriental clothes and the Arab man. Yet this episode has even more layers, which I also described in the book: a few weeks after our walk in the suburbs of Fuengirola I had a vision one night while we were sitting together in conversation in Calle's living room.

There, I experienced the same scene from the perspective of the Arab man. Simultaneously, and somehow in slow motion, something in me started to argue what I knew to be true: I was seeing myself and Calle through the eyes of a former incarnation of mine.

"I then turn around to look for Ishatar but I cannot see her. At one of the stalls, I spot a manuscript so beautifully made that I linger for a while admiring it. As I'm about to pick it up I am overwhelmed by a strong feeling. An inexplicable certainty makes me leave it where it is and walk on. Driven by unknown forces I'm moved along by the throng of people into a state of mind which suddenly changes everything. Two men are talking to each other at a distance from me. It is as my reality is torn apart. I am rooted to the spot. I have a feeling that I know them, but I don't know from where. Now, one of them turns and spots me. His eyes shine like the sun and burn with fire. He is pointing at me. Are they men of the Inquisition? I feel panic spreading in me. I have no intention of waiting to find out who they are. I start running. Back to Ishatar's house. I see nothing. Bump into everything. I hear a voice calling out my name. Ishatar's voice? I cannot even calm down when I'm in Ishatar's cool room with the door closed behind me."

Calle's sublime contact and manoeuvrability in the ether enabled him to activate these past events. In the same way, it is possible to gain insight into future events. Neither future nor past are "far away". They are always accessible and can be manifested instantaneously.

Another episode described in the book is my confrontation with a bull. Calle led me into Malaga's bullring, where he left me standing in the centre of the plaza of death while he himself walked toward the gate through which the bulls enter the arena. I didn't suspect a thing and thought he was playing a joke on me. But suddenly a huge bull emerges from the dark shadows of the gate. He spots me and starts running toward me. I stand paralyzed at first, then try to run away, but my shoes slip on the yellow gravel. A few seconds feel like an eternity. The bull is right in front of me and just before it is about to impale me, I hear a voice inside me say: "Meet me. Fear not. Meet me!" At that moment, I step forward toward the bull, which runs straight through me without causing the slightest damage. Afterwards, I collapse, completely exhausted from the tension.

As we left the arena and sat down at a table in an outdoor café, Calle told me what he had just staged and why. The bull symbolized my projections of dominance and fear that I had created over time. The confrontation with the bull and my courage to face it dissolved these shadows that were rooted in past judgements and prejudices.

We all share in the atrocities that are happening everywhere. They are the fruit of our negative projections. Through Calle's and my previous practices of synchronizing us, it was possible for him to project this event into the shared etheric field we had created together, so that I perceived it as a real physical event.

Through training we will gain access to our innate intuitive sensitivity. We will develop a recognition of the multidimensional layers in any situation and sense when there is noise on the line. If a person tells me something, I can usually sense right away if it's true or not. But only if I can avoid being biased or judgemental. Then my discernment remains intact. This applies not only in one-on-one situations, but also on a collective level.

In a situation where I am faced with someone who, for whatever reason, cannot be truthful, I would neither condemn them, nor would I try to challenge their behaviour and share my insight. But I might avoid having too much to do with such a person. Only if it is someone with whom I have a close or intimate relationship will I acknowledge the experience in my field and find a way of relating and communicating through the wisdom of my heart. Of course, this is not always possible as untruths can be perceived as shadows that cause feelings of betrayal and loss of faith, which in turn cause grief.

Loneliness and unity

Maybe that's why I've always felt lonely here in physical existence. Throughout my life, I've made a few attempts to create a family or enter into a deeper, intimate relationship, but each time it has more or less failed. Witnessing myself writing these words, I notice the tone of self-judgement and justification. Why do I question the very fabric of my life? A quiet voice rises within me: *If it is not failure, what else would it be?* Crossings of destined paths? Communion of Selves? Spiritual Growing? Karmic bonds forming and releasing themselves? Shared tasks and inspirations? Gatherings of experience and insights? *Be still.* The edgy feeling of doom disappears. *Only you can know.*

I've had relationships with some amazing women, smart, wise and beautiful, but when I've tried to be who I am, it somehow has never been conducive to the relationships. *But who else were you then, if not yourself?* Good question. Have I ever been myself? For many years I tried to find my place in the world but realized that it was impossible for me to live up to other people's ideas of who I was or how they wanted me to be. And even though I saw through the ideas and projections, I retreated into myself rather than confronted the problem. I retreated and closed my inner doors rather than opening myself toward a confrontation that I believed would lead to no solution. Yet at the same time I always stayed available for the possibility of change. I had come to the conclusion that I have always belonged to God and therefore no one belonged to me. In that belief, my former rigid views on God meet with my understanding of God as Consciousness and as the only present, only possible, all-harmonious expression of life. Reflecting on my countless experiences with the field of Divine harmony, it is a challenge for me to realize that the cause of the existential loneliness that has followed me through life is my longing to belong to another human being who belongs to me.

When I am able to transform loneliness, even in the moments when I feel most cut off from others, it is possible to step into the Oneness where we all belong. This loneliness was also Calle's lot, and I often wonder how many others might feel the same way? Is it a common human condition? This heart-crushing pain when you figuratively and literally stand naked in front of another person who cannot or will not see – neither you nor themselves. When you thought you had given everything, had completely revealed yourself, unlocked all the closed doors to the other and walked through them together, but then that last door just won't open. Instead, you step into an unfathomable void. You feel confronted with a seemingly endless horizon of disconnectedness stretched out far and wide toward you, which seems to have manifested an insurmountable distance to the true and only thing that matters in any relationship: daring to stand together authentically, unveiled, in equality and God Consciousness.

Solitude and unity in the Bridal Chamber

Even in the intimate meeting in the Bridal Chamber, the distance to the other can be insurmountable. If the urges are unleashed without the souls being united, loneliness can be paralyzing. If there is no true devotion in the meeting, this only leads to guilt and loss. Two people who do not truly love and respect each other should perhaps think twice before entering the Bridal Chamber together. In the *Gospel of Philip* we can find three essential statements about the sacredness of deep companionship and sexuality:

"Sexual union *(koinonia)* between two unequal partners is inappropriate."

"Even the worldly embrace is a mystery; and even more mysterious is the embrace which embodies the hidden union. It is not merely the reality of the flesh, for there is silence in that embrace. It does not arise from a random impulse or from desire, it is the result of will (conscious presence/awareness). It is not of darkness, but of Light."

"Faith *(pistis)* is to receive and love *(agape)* is to give. No one can receive without faith and no one can give without love. We believe and are therefore able to receive; we give to experience love. Those who give without love experience nothing of interest."

The moment one of the lovers is not true, not faith-filled, there is no equality. Faith must be divided into Heavenly and worldly faith. Heavenly faith is the knowledge and awareness of the presence of divine harmony or Oneness. Worldly faith is the presence of the heart and dedication of the self toward another person, belief or task. When there is no consciousness present in the meeting of two partners, when one party has lost heavenly faith in their own connection to God Consciousness or worldly faith in the other because he or she gives and receives without true love, then the interaction will be loveless and will have a subversive effect on the parties. In every true friendship and in every intimate meeting between two lovers, the conscious embrace, as I see it, is the most important and the prerequisite for the relationship as a whole. Only then comes the kiss.

The unfolding of the libido is a natural part of being human but is also a great challenge. Therefore, the libido's fulfilment must be connected to the heart. This is often not possible during puberty, when the sexual force can be so overwhelming that it just needs to be released. The development of empathy and compassion, presence and sensory awareness should therefore be the most important part of any sexual education, which all too often becomes an introduction to pure physical mechanics.

Reading the future

When Calle attested that he was able to change a person's life trajectory, it was because he could see the long-term effect of the client's current actions. In the moment of his consultation and healing he changed their attitude by working with their Light Body so that the future picture he saw had less chance of becoming reality.

Basically, it's very simple: if you are a smoker and want to avoid lung problems in twenty years, one of the first things to do would be to quit buying cigarettes and stop smoking now. If you are afraid of being isolated or alone later in life, start to relate lovingly to every person you meet. In the same way, humanity can avoid any future disasters or severe challenges if we change our behaviour now. The problem is that most people think that it's only all the other people who should change their habits and behaviour – *it will be okay if I make a little mess here and there, as long as it's just once in a while. I by myself cannot change things anyway.* And that's exactly how we repeatedly miss the mark.

You could say that predicting certain scenarios is fairly straightforward if you familiarize yourself with the current prevailing imbalances that are likely to cause diseases or disasters at a later date. But in my experience, my visions have never been based on logical conclusions, but on an intuitive certainty. Often, however, these visions have left me with doubts, not so much about their accuracy, but more about whether I should share them. Issues of polluted drinking water, the rise of profit-based medical industries, dystopian societies and corrupt political systems don't sound too inspirational. How can sharing such information help? Many a time I was called out quite aggressively, so I have been searching for ways to reach people without fuelling their flames and stirring up these backlashes. I never had a problem with being confrontational when I believed that a topic or a situation was important to voice, but there is a big difference between confrontation and provocation. If someone feels provoked, they will not move one inch from their point of view, the distance between us becomes even bigger, the walls of separation even higher. But why then did these visions come to me? Were they only a confirmation of the existence of our multidimensional consciousness? Or were they a call to action that I had the responsibility to share, no matter the consequences?

While living on Samsø, I had a very strong connection to the island's nature. Much of the land is cultivated farmland there. The drinking water was not very good back then, even though the water boards claimed otherwise. Unfortunately, the people in charge were farmers themselves, so there was a conflict of interest. This is the situation in most of Denmark. As long as you avoided measuring for toxins that you knew for sure would show critical levels, you could claim year after year that Danish drinking water was the best in the world. Nowadays, the toxins have reached the groundwater, and this is the biggest environmental disaster of all. Pure ground water has healing properties. When we try to chemically purify contaminated water, we destroy its structure and its healing properties. Last year I shared a video on my YouTube channel, in which I showed how we are able to change the frequency of the water directly from the tap.

The belief, promotion or suggestion that it is possible to "treat" our fields with toxic chemicals, and later on "fix" nature if it was poisoned by the "treatment" fits perfectly with the horrendous fallacy that arrived in the world as a seemingly logical concept in the late 1950s and early 1960s, when all kinds of chemistry became part of humanity's everyday life: tinned fresh air or furniture and carpet sprays, various hair and cosmetic preparations, detergents and cleansers, toxic plastic packaging, poisonous coatings on kitchenware, harmful paint or building materials, heavy metals like lead and chromium in clothing dyes and synthetic fabric of shoes and clothes, etcetera. Every day we are confronted with a seemingly endless series of scandals while chemical factories simply move to new locations when the environmental burden becomes too great to bear, but without cleaning up after themselves. All these atrocities and offences are the results of irresponsible actions of these companies as well as our choices to use these products.

The whole mindset has spread to most major industries, for example to the pharmaceutical industry. Here the profits are so high that these companies are among the richest in the world. A huge part of their astronomical profit is possible because some of them compromise on ethics and morals to such an extent that they behave like mafias that pay off their crimes. And as long as there are enough doctors, scientists, healthcare institutions and politicians willing to compromise their integrity for mammon, this system will not only continue but grow. The only solution is for us, the citizens of the world, to stand up and take responsibility for our own lives now. What products are we buying, what information do we believe? The challenge is our own convenience and our dependence on comfort and security. But comfort and security can be overpriced. Especially when they will ultimately cause the loss of freedom we like to praise so highly.

Our life here on Earth is, from a universal perspective, just a brief moment. Therefore, we need to ask ourselves the questions: If not us, who? If not now, when? And in the mirror of these questions, we will find our own worldly responsibilities of being ourselves the change we want to see in the world, as well as our Divine gifts and heritage that will help us to live that change.

15

THE MUSIC OF HEAVEN AND EARTH

**You know you belong
when your heart sings a song**

When you are completely silent, especially if you are spending time in nature, you can sometimes pick up a sound, an all-embracing ethereal whisper that, once you hear it, never disappears. This sound is a universal harmonious continuum of all notes and tones, of their sound as well as their structure, and we are positively affected by it whether we can hear it or not. Only when we fill the ether with disturbing thought forms and judgemental words, our sense of hearing on both the physical and etheric planes hardens to such an extent that we lose connection to this healing sound of the universe. Through communal toning, singing, prayer and invocations, as well as making or listening to music that has a cleansing and heart-opening effect on us, we are able to reconnect with this continuum of healing.

It wasn't before midlife that I became aware of how we are connected through sound. But from my earliest childhood it was Bach, Handel, Haydn, Mozart and Beethoven who spoke to me, and today I know that many of their works purify the ether and maintain our connection to the cosmic sound.

The first piece of music I created was a hymn composed on the Castello harmonica Uncle Hans had given me. It was a simple melody and lyrics that described my retreats in the forests outside Aarhus and the experiences and emotions I had gone through in Varde. I only vaguely remember the feeling of a slow melody moving between suspended chords and the dissolution of these, on top of a ground of open fifths. Back in 1963, I wasn't consciously aware of the "right" way of combining chords, I just put them together by ear and intuition. Only in recent years did I begin to understand what the use of open fifths entails and why they have a heart-opening effect.

Open fifths open up locked areas of the human heart, mind and soul. When the fifths form the basis of melodies that spring from the true heart of the composer, the emotions of those present at a concert where such music and songs are performed are being released. Being in the same space where the music and song are expressed can have a healing effect, lifting the fallen and bringing detached people back to their true identity. In a concert situation, sound unfolds freely in space and is therefore liberating. The voices can move between major and minor without any hindrance, even creating interference when a more insistent opening sound for a traumatized person is needed.

When I started working with the basic musical archetypal elements and geometric shapes of open chords in various keys, I realized that this is a very effective way to reach people's hearts. It's not just a question of technical ability, but of the aim and direction of the music and lyrics. And the direction always depends on the intentions of the composer and lyricist and the feelings and emotions from which the work originates. Another important aspect is the performer's state of mind on stage or in the studio. The focus should never be on performance. The singer and musician must *be* the song. Then it's not a question of the technical ability of the singer or musician, but only of his or her integrity and sincerity. This creates access to inspiration and healing for those attending the concert. The quality of a voice that is free from the need to show off or pretend to be something it is not will reach so much deeper, transforming traumatized emotions in the process, reaching higher frequencies and developing clarified feelings.

Anyone who has participated in a communal toning session and felt at ease and able to surrender and dissolve into the wholeness of the harmonies, has experienced how the sound suddenly amplifies, as if the choir has been doubled. This is a sign that contact has been made with the ethereal tone, with its all-encompassing harmony. Over and over, I have experienced how the activated Light Beings in the ether become visible. I don't know to which hierarchies these Angels belong, only that they bring deep peace, healing and hope. I perceive them as responses to the harmonics we create during toning, which are like lights we switch on and connect us to the higher frequencies of the ether.

An Indian harmonium is a veritable cornucopia of overtones. I was lucky enough to be led to get to know this wonderful instrument of transformation and healing at an event I had helped to organize for the charity Hearts and Hands in 2002. One of the performers at the concert, an Indian singer, was in possession of a small selection of these amazing instruments and saw my enthusiasm for one of them, which he allowed me to buy. Since then, I have acquired different versions of the instrument. Each one of them has its own identity and sound signature.

A harmonium requires no electricity or internet; one hand is operating the bellows while the other plays the mini keyboard.

Learning to express yourself on the instrument between pianissimo and forte, as well as creating a smooth sustaining sound, is almost like expressing yourself with your own voice. There is something very moving in the experience that one has to initiate the "breath" of the instrument with one's hand. And the more conscious we are about our own breath in connection to our movement, the more harmonic resonance will be created in the sound. In the beginning, the music that came through when I sat with the harmonium was almost always based on open chords and especially open fifths, allowing the voice to be free and to fly high without being bound by major or minor.

The birth of a song can take many forms. Sometimes it just appears in one instant, and at other times it feels like a whole process needs to happen before the song will fully show itself. A process in which I, or those close to me, have to shift or grow in awareness before the song can truly arrive and can find a form that feels complete.

During different talks and workshops, a little melody appeared while we were toning. It kept coming back, always accompanied by a frequency that was somehow moving almost everyone in the room to tears. One day at a workshop in the south of Germany, it appeared again, and suddenly I heard my voice sing: "Maria, Maria, Maria, Maria, Maria – Mariam Mare, Mariam Mare, Maria." An instant before the words came, I knew it was a hymn to the Master Mariam Magdalene. But something was still missing. The song was somehow unfulfilled. And no matter what I tried in the next weeks and months, I couldn't find a way to break through and reach what I felt was wanting to express itself.

It took a whole year before the song finally continued its download. I was home alone for three days and decided to set up one of my digital keyboards in front of my altar, which was arranged in a small, deep windowsill in my office. On the altar was the icon of the Madonna of the Broken Heart that I had received at Saydnaya Monastery during a trip to Syria in 2003.[22] The icon was printed on a piece of cardboard that a young novice from the monastery had picked up from the floor, where it lay broken in half, right through the heart of the Madonna. The novice had glued the pieces together,

---

[22] A documentary in Danish, *Syrien – Den Skjulte Virkelighed (Syria – The Hidden Reality),* about this trip was filmed by Danish National Television and can be seen on YouTube.

made a beautiful frame for it, and chose a place on the wall of a side corridor where it had hung undisturbed for 50 years. The head of the convent, Sister Theodore, saw how taken I was with the icon and she took it off the nail and presented it to me with the words:

"If you will take good care of her, she will take good care of you."

It turned out that it was Sister Theodore who, as a young novice, had assembled the pieces of cardboard and made the icon, which she now entrusted to my care. I was both moved and deeply grateful. The next day I visited the stigmata Myrna of Soufanieh in Damascus, who blessed the icon in her chapel. After the ceremony, Myrna suddenly exclaimed: "Smell, it smells of roses!"

It did, so much so that the whole chapel room in her flat was filled with the most delightful scent of roses.

Now I was sitting in front of the Madonna of the Broken Heart and I had just switched on my keyboard, which somehow was set to the sound of a string ensemble. Without any thought, I put my hands on the keys and started singing the Mariam Mare song.[23] After the first part that I already knew, the song moved into a new section all by itself, which turned out to be what I had felt the song was missing. It felt like slowly being moved within a completely open space. I was present at the Crucifixion two thousand years ago, and now I heard myself singing to Mariam Magdalene:

"I saw you there standing,
trembling by the Cross,
you were the thunder and the lightning,
that ripped the veil apart,

[23]   The process can be seen on YouTube in *The Coming of the Divine Feminine and Mariam Mare, A Song of Healing.*

in the Holy of the Holies,
you were opening our hearts."

The following repeated "Maria, Maria ..." part felt like the most soothing and transformational force, leading me to continue with a second verse:

"I saw you there holding,
that wounded bird in your hand,
saw the tears you were hiding,
as you healed it by your command.
It was not for him you were crying,
it was for us."

With these additions, the song had now taken on a completely different character. The tempo was slower and my voice felt differently present. I decided to move the keyboard back to the living room where our small home studio was located. I wanted to record the song as close to its download and as present to the connection with its source as possible. While recording, a lamp in the living room suddenly started flashing every time I sang the new piece. I checked the bulb, but it was adjusted correctly.

This was repeated when Githa came home a few days later and sang two beautiful parts to the song. Every time such a process with a song has happened it feels completely unreal. How can music just appear from one moment to the next, as if it has fallen down from the heavens into one's consciousness and manifest when the time is right – and then later be shared and sung by people all over the world? This song truly has a life of its own. It tells what was happening during the Crucifixion at the moment when Yeshua united his spirit with the highest aspects of consciousness. The ultimate way of giving IT UP. It was the moment a lightning bolt struck in the innermost part of the Temple, the Holy of Holies, where only the High Priest was allowed once a year on the Day of Atonement. Now the curtain was torn, and the sanctuary was accessible to all.

This symbolizes the opening of the hardened hearts of humankind. Now the innermost heart chamber was open, and Mariam stood at the foot of the Cross with the wounded bird, the pain and darkness of humankind in her hand, and healed it with the power of her love while tears of release, compassion and care for us, humanity, were streaming down her face. It was not for Yeshua she wept. She was part of the task they fulfilled together in their incarnation: the removal of the lower vibrations within the etheric layers of the human collective consciousness.

Another song that came in a similar way, with delayed sequences triggered by different frequencies of people and places, is the hymn *May God Bless You.*[24] The first part arrived like the verses of *Mariam Mare*. One day after, while I was sitting at the piano, it appeared just like that: Here I am – sing me.

> "May God Bless You
> And your loved ones
> May His Light shine
> On you always."

I recorded it on my phone and sent it to Naleea, as we were preparing to include different songs in the German workshops. Three months later, while we were working on the edit of *The God Formula* together, I suddenly received a verse to the song:

> "There's a Light that shines forever
> Hidden deep within our hearts
> And every breath we take is sacred
> Feel its Presence in this Now!"

---

[24] Hear the song in the video *May God Bless You* on YouTube.

But I knew there was still one verse missing, and it was impossible for me to get any closer. I had sent the verse to Naleea and within an hour, she sent back the following:

"There's a song that sounds forever
All the way through space and time
Hear it calling, feel it falling
From your heart right into mine."

At the recording of the song, Githa added a beautiful intuitive voice, while the final chorus "Malkoota – Hallelujah – Ahava – Hallelujah" was sung by Peleh Ben-David and Lars Kiehn.

Later I sent the song to a circle of friends around the world, including musician Jet in Africa, Ib Asmussen in Viborg, Beach Boy Al Jardine in Big Sur, Kasper Winding, Simone Bendix and their two children in Paris, Edward and his wife in the Faroe Islands, Tinne Stender and Niels Fabæk in Aalborg, Gail Swanson and her grandson Elijah in Florida, Martin Delfs and his family in Copenhagen, Jaap in the Netherlands, Hanna Snorridottir in Iceland, Frances in England, Noé and Amelie Hauschildt in Montpellier, Diane Soa in Copenhagen, to Jesper Roland in Valby, who also edited the video, and of course to Naleea in Hamburg. Everyone involved brought their own unique energy to the field of the song and it's one of the most beautiful musical experiences I've had in my life.

Now, years later, *May God Bless You* has developed again. One day at a rehearsal for an upcoming concert, while Naleea and I were about to sing the line "May His Light shine", it was like scales falling from our eyes. We have been speaking and writing so much about God being Consciousness, not a male figure! But although the term and concept of *the Beloved Father* creates a very powerful frequency field, we wanted to dedicate everything we do to finding new ways and words of expression for the Consciousness of the All-Harmonious in a way beyond duality. "His Light" became "the Light". And some weeks later the field of the boys from Daisy,

192

with whom I have been rehearsing the song as well, led us to connect the final chorus to the activating frequencies of the I AM:

"Shine Your Light – Shining Bright – Heart of Mine – Let it Shine."

Another great experience that opened through the power of sound happened when I took part in a documentary film about the Aramaic language that was shot in Israel in 2014, singing the ancient Fire Chariot practice *B'Shm Adonai* in the famous Cave 4 in Qumran by the Dead Sea in Israel, close to the ruins of the University of the Essenes.[25] Cave 4 is the cave where the most scrolls were found, which were placed there in haste because it was closest to the university itself. The Essenes who were in the university at the time had to flee in a hurry as Roman soldiers were approaching to avenge the Jewish revolt that ended in the total destruction of both the university at Qumran and nearly all of Jerusalem.

Cave 4 was a very special cave. As mentioned earlier, it was originally used as an initiation site where the aspirant would spend *40 days in the desert*, alone and fasting. In the psychology of the Aramaic language, *being in the desert* is a metaphor for a state of consciousness. An unprotected state. All layers of the personality come to the surface and must be both met and transformed with an attitude of unwavering devotion and trust. You are stripped naked and have made yourself accessible, so God can find you. Achieving this consciousness was the main purpose and desired state of this trial. When you go into the desert, there is nowhere to hide. And as we can read in the New Testament, after a while in this state, Yeshua was surrounded by the wild animals of the desert, which meant that he had to face his own shadows.

---

[25] You can watch the whole process in the video *The Gate of Light* on YouTube.

In the end, we read that Satan appears and tries to tempt Yeshua to give up his endeavour. So, Yeshua had to deal with his own ego with all its subversive strategies, and as we can read, Yeshua succeeded in his initiation, and immediately afterwards he went to Canaan to marry his beloved.

I had visited the cave a few times before and knew that it was quite difficult to climb up there because everything you walk on or try to hold on to is so porous that you can very easily lose your grip and fall.

When photographer Ami Shamir and I finally entered the cave, I sat down with my tambourine and started singing myself into the trance that is necessary for the practice to succeed. I needed time to distance myself from the recording situation, but slowly my divided focus unified into a field of neutralizing or nullifying energy. The experience was intense. I'm not sure at what point in the process, which lasted well over an hour, I lost contact with my surroundings and had the feeling of being lifted out of my body and out of the cave, floating into a sphere of acceptance and healing Light. When I eventually returned to the cave, I was surrounded by old brothers from my time as an Essene at Qumran University 2,000 years ago. I opened my eyes and found the entire cave completely illuminated. A deep sense of gratitude filled my entire being.

The director Ole Bernt Frøshaug, who had stayed back at the foot of the plateau below the cave because he had broken an arm, had heard a thunderous sound from the Qumran valley that turned out to be the wingbeats of 12 doves flying up past the entrance to Cave 4, which he experienced as a blessing, connecting Heaven and Earth. Despite his plaster arm, he found the strength and balance to climb up to the entrance of the cave. There was no way he would have stayed down there on his own. He needed to share his powerful experience with Ami and I, who were sitting silently inside, bathed in Light. All three of us were shaken to the core. Ami was the one to break the silence. To him, it was clear that we were here for a purpose, at the right time in the right place, experiencing this apparition of cosmic Light Structures and Angelic Frequencies.

This changed everything. Nothing we recorded afterwards could say more than the words of this 3,000-year-old song, sung in the cave that psychologist and seer Helen Schucman, who channelled *A Course in Miracles,* had seen in a vision and which, when she visited the cave in 1973, she believed was the most sacred place in the world. As witnessed by her friend Kenneth Wapnick, Helen was not one to show her feelings easily. But when she came to Qumran and was standing before Cave 4 she started to cry, announcing that this was the cave from her vision in which she saw an ancient scroll with "GOD IS" written on it.

Before my experience in the cave, the Welsh seer Carol Clarke had predicted that there was a cave in the Holy Land where a transformation awaited me. When the film documenting the experience was completed, I sent it to her. Subsequently, I received this email from her:

"Dear Lars,

This is the most beautiful and moving film; the cave is exactly as I 'saw' during the reading I did for you, and as I watched, chills ran down my spine. You found your true self in this cave, you became as you were two thousand years ago, I could see the transformation within you and you were surrounded by fourteen people/ beings as you sat there. Time, (if there is such a thing), ran backwards and I saw you in different clothing, with a pure golden energy surrounding you. What could be described as an angel sat by your side and the others sat in a semi-circle around you. The one who baptized you sat directly in front of you, connecting with your energy, you were joined as one.

This place above all places must confirm to you, who you are. Tears fell from my eyes as I watched, for you had come to the place that was most important to you in that lifetime, a place where you understood all things and it prepared you for the path ahead.

Thank you for sharing this with me, I feel so moved by the beauty of it. The music was incredible and inspiring.

With much love and gratitude
Carol"

Described as an intellectual, pragmatic and grounded person, Helen Schucman emphasized on several occasions that the physical world is in many ways deceptive and seductive, and that it is in visions that we must see true reality. Like Yeshua, she advocated that only a child is able to see through the illusions of this world. There would be just one lesson that we would need to learn here: to stand firm in this consciousness of the pure and fearless child – with an attitude toward life that is free of any worry – and truly realize that *illusions are illusions*. They have no power whatsoever over us.

May this chapter about the power of sound, belonging and transformation end with the most profound quote from the kabbalistic scripture *The Zohar*, about the power and purpose of music expressed in a single sentence:

"There are places in Heaven that are
only open to the voice of song."

16

THE GATE OF NEW BEGINNINGS

Then there was peace, love …

In the Western world, there is one topic that we prefer not to talk about: death and the process of dying! It's as if we've completely forgotten that one day we'll leave here. And this is despite the fact that the only thing we know for sure when a new human being is born is that he or she will eventually depart from the physical world again. But we don't talk about it.

From my experience of working with the dying in hospices and from working with Calle, who was monitoring that the transfer process of a dying or deceased person went harmoniously and well almost daily, I know that this alienation toward death often leads to some heartbreaking situations. I once experienced a family member telling a woman who was in the very end of the dying process that she still had many good years to look forward to. To the grief and despair of the family member, the woman drew her last breath a few minutes later. Such incidents are most tragic because it is the dying person who has to suffer from attitudes of ignorance or pretence, which bring tension, sadness and alienation instead of the intended comfort. Many times, I have witnessed a dying person being unsettled and disturbed by well-meaning relatives. Therefore, in the following, I will try to give an idea of how the process of dying unfolds and how it can be accompanied. Firstly, for older people who have reached the point in their incarnation when the "fruit is ripe" and death is a natural occurrence in that chapter of their life; then for those who have arrived at the final period of a serious illness; and lastly, what happens when death comes unexpectedly and suddenly. We have gathered together the essence of many books and studies, including the several thousand near-death stories collected by Dr Raymond Moody, as well as Naleea's and my own experiences.

In old age or as the culmination of a period of serious illness, the process of dying begins with fatigue, where sleep slowly overtakes wakefulness. No solid food is consumed as hunger is no longer felt. From there on, a gradual dissolution of the elements of creation, earth, water, air and fire, begins.[26]

In the first stage, when the earth element dissolves, the external signs are that the dying person's body becomes thinner and weaker, while internally, the third eye is being activated. There are short moments of out-of-body experiences or a "blending" of reality, where a person can see glimpses of different layers of the etheric fields with their inner sight. The people I have been sitting with told me about visions of archetypal figures, often of a religious nature. It can be challenging for both the person as well as their relatives and friends, if the person shares their experiences. Often, the relatives would reject such visions, as usually no one else is able to see what they are perceiving, judging those reports from the other side as being made up in confusion or putting them down to the side effects of medication.

I never initiate a conversation with the dying person but stay attentive and listening to what they share or want to express. Sometimes I might ask what it is the person is seeing or experiencing if they start to describe something but seem to find no further words. If they are not ready to share

[26] See the little booklet *Preparing for Death and Helping the Dying* by Sangye Khadro, which I can highly recommend.

anything although I am aware that they had contact with the other side, I stay silent and connect with them through their heart space or a part of their Light Body to which my attention is being drawn. This process of suddenly being confronted with a reality that no one else seems to be aware of can cause confusion and make it difficult for the dying person to distinguish between the known and familiar reality and the unknown fields of consciousness they are now experiencing.

The second stage involves the dissolution of the water element; the outward signs are that one's body is getting lighter as the fluids are drying up, while inside one has a perception of smoke. I have even experienced a faint scent of smoke detectable in the air around a dying person's bed. He or she has long since stopped taking in any nourishment but needs fluids to moisten their mouth and lips. Any touch that is exchanged needs to be even softer now, and only in agreement with the person. If there is a need for hygiene procedures, you have to make sure that there is ample time and that the atmosphere is soothing and peaceful, especially when there is shame about not being able to control the release of urine and stool anymore. Be ready to take their hand if they wish you to. Always be gentle and hold space for any emotion or projection, any painful belief or memory to surface.

The fire element dissolves in the third stage; the external sign is that the heat and digestive power of the body decline, and internally one perceives visions of sparks. Feel the change in the pulse of the Light Body. Never "push" any specific energy into their field as an attempt to help them. Just witness the energies of their physical body becoming fainter and finer and connect through the heart in communion. If you perceive their hands or body to be slightly cold, check if the person needs the warmth and coziness of a shawl or a blanket. Do not automatically pull it over them, as they might feel good in that temperature and the weight of a blanket can feel suffocating.

In the fourth stage, when the wind or air element dissolves, the external signs are that breathing becomes heavy and irregular until it ceases in a final exhalation. In the Buddhist tradition it is said that internally you have a vision of a flame that is getting smaller and smaller. Essential oils like rose, lavender, frankincense, myrrh and spikenard can be very supportive especially at this part of the dying process. But it is important to feel the receptivity of the person. Always check with them if they like the smell. Gently show them the oil with an open lid and slowly draw the bottle nearer to their nose.

While some might love to be surrounded closely by these essences, either in a fragrance lamp, a diffuser or directly applied on their heart space, their forehead, under their collarbones, on the area of their kidneys or on their inner wrists, others might only feel comfort from the presence of these smells and frequencies from a distant corner of the room.

If the breathing becomes heavy and difficult, connect through blessing and prayer to the highest transformational field of love and peace you are able to reach. Call in the Angels and Light Beings from both the person and yourself, and ask for their help, and you will both feel a release. Ask for transformation of all unresolved topics and keep being connected with the Presence of the All-Harmonious Consciousness and the frequency of Grace.

When the breathing has stopped, when the dissolving of the elements has been completed and when there is no longer any movement in the brain or circulation, the dying is declared clinically dead. However, death has not yet occurred as long as consciousness is still present in the body. In many religious and spiritual traditions, the ceremony of the wake that lasts for three days and nights has been established as a way of safeguarding that the consciousness of a family member or friend will not be disturbed through any interference on the physical body. Calle would always work with the dying in the days before their departure and then again three days afterwards.

The last of the five senses to shut down is the sense of hearing. This is important to know as I have seen family members who, believing that death had occurred and that the deceased was no longer present, have argued loudly about who was entitled to inherit this or that, not realizing that the dying person is actually still present and can perceive what is going on. Timing of organ removal is a very controversial topic in regard to sensory awareness after the declaration of brain death, and I recommend thorough research on organ donation if that is a subject for consideration.

Throughout the whole dying process, the person often sees deceased family members gather around the deathbed as well as their Guardian Angel. Sometimes Yeshua, Mother Mary or other religious Archetypal Beings appear. These manifest to reassure the dying person and to help them with the transition. Sometimes the dying person may make sounds as attempts of responding to situations or Beings they are perceiving, which can be misinterpreted by those present as the person speaking in delirium or out of pain.

It's also important to realize that many a time, family members are the biggest obstacle to a smooth and harmonic dying process. When family members are scared and don't know what to do, or when they hold on to the dying person because they don't allow themselves to let the person go, what often happens is that the dying person tries to "pull themselves together" and fulfil the wishes of their relatives out of consideration for them. Sometimes, the relatives' fear of the unknown is transferred to the dying person. In such circumstances, it would be much better for the dying person to be in the care of a knowledgeable and compassionate hospice worker who knows the process and therefore knows what to do. To me there is no doubt, that if the relatives or friends close to the dying would be able to have a calm and relaxed attitude built on trust, this would be the optimal situation.

Gentle music and singing can have a calming effect, especially if songs are sung or played that have been meaningful in the dying person's life. You can also sit close to the dying person's ear and quietly recite a soothing text, prayer or song.

Physical contact with the dying person can have a liberating effect, when it is guided by unconditional love and intuition. Only through a loving and intuitive presence and attention can we sense their true personal needs or wishes. The *Rukha* Practice, as well as the *Butterfly Hands* Practice, both passed on in Chapter 18, will be extremely useful in any phase of the death process.

In most near-death experiences, consciousness leaves the body immediately, without the slow process of the dissolution of the physical elements. We hear many reports of people who come back to their incarnation after they are declared dead, how they suddenly find themselves floating at the ceiling and watching themselves lying on their deathbed. They hear the doctor informing those present about their death and see and feel the grief of their relatives.

If a person's destiny is to leave their present lifetime, it would be very helpful if those present gather around the deathbed and, for example, hold hands. Standing closely together will not only console the relatives, affirming the love they all share, it will also help the person to leave with more ease, as they will feel the frequencies of love and gratitude, instead of feeling bound by sadness. At some point, a family member or friend may gently ask the dying person to let go, while everyone maintains and radiates an open and peaceful attitude. This can be followed by a hymn or a soothing tone or a song.

When you actively participate in the dying person's transition from the physical to the spiritual world, sometimes an etheric field opens around the dying, allowing those present to "see" the dying person's Light Body and the Light Beings present on the etheric plane with the physical eyes. It is a deeply moving experience that gives anyone who witnesses it an insight into how beautiful and filled with peace and love this passage is. When we are able to accept the process and have trust that this natural transition from one reality to another is being supervised from the other side too, we can perceive a feeling of hands holding each other across the tides between Heaven and Earth, insuring a safe journey for the deceased. After such an experience you will no longer fear death because you understand that this process can be compared to the caterpillar that thinks the end has come, only to realize moments later that it has transformed into a butterfly. A very important and helpful handbook for anyone who wants to know more about how we can be of assistance in a caring way to the dying is Felicity Warner's brilliant work *Soul Midwives*, which I highly recommend.

Many who have returned from "the dead" report the confusion of experiencing themselves as still being present and "alive", but without being in their physical body. We hear fascinating stories about instant journeys to a beloved person or place by the power of thought. This phase takes a different length of "time" for different people, depending on their knowledge about the death process as well as their mental and emotional state. At some point, the perceived surroundings fade into a seemingly impenetrable darkness, which can be perceived as very frightening. Some feel it as an emotional darkness of despair, some experience it as dreary landscapes in which they find themselves walking through muddy soil. For others, it is a neutral darkness in which they feel somehow released from some parts of their identity. But at one point, no matter what form this phase has taken, the thousands of people who came back from the other side report the very same occurrence as the next step: from somewhere a Light will appear. The most common description is that a corridor or tunnel suddenly opens up, at the end of which an all-consuming Light can be seen. Here, the experience of having helpers in the form of Light Beings becomes a living part of the new reality. It is on the journey through this tunnel that moving images of our life pass by as a form of a review. The consciousness of the deceased is confronted with everything they have experienced in the incarnation. There is no judgement or punishment involved, just an experience in which the consciousness understands and sees the life that has just passed with complete clarity.

Much confusion and fear in this whole process could be avoided if the consciousness, while incarnated, had been enlightened about the different stages of the death process and what a significant initiation into the beautiful spheres of reality beyond the earthly experiences it actually is. Countless people who have had near-death experiences report that peace and unconditional love enfolds and surrounds them in the spiritual world so strongly that they have no wish to leave these realms. When the Being of Light that has accompanied the deceased tells them that they still have something to do in their earthly life and therefore must return to their body, it often causes reluctance to leave this wonderful place. Later, when the temporarily deceased has returned to the body and their incarnation, the experience has usually triggered a completely new outlook on life. There is now an understanding and willingness to live their life on an entirely new basis, with no desire to waste the remaining time on trivial things and chores. Often, a deep wish and a clear vision of how to be of service to others has surfaced, which sometimes includes communicating what they had experienced. Death is no longer a threat, but rather a door to a different part of our consciousness once we have lived through and collected the experiences we had planned to have in our current incarnation.

If death comes unexpectedly, such as in a road accident, where there is no time for the aforementioned process of the unravelling of the elements, it often leaves the deceased in great confusion about what has just happened. The consciousness is convinced that it is still incarnated as it can follow everything that happens around the earthly body it has just left. It recognizes that it is "alive" but is not aware that it is no longer part of the physical realm. It tries to talk to people or travels by thought to places it liked. So much confusion in that state of the death process could be avoided if the deceased had been receiving information at an early stage of their life about what it means to leave physical reality.

People who have taken their own life are confronted with their action and realize that it has not solved any problems, but only created more than they already had. It is an expensive experience of stagnation that will cause in equal measure stagnation in the spiritual world until they fully understand the implications of the action for all involved, as well as how the ego's desires and self-created suffering must be transformed into the Higher Self's compassion and unconditional love for all living things, including themselves.

There is no death as most people have come to understand it. Eternal darkness is an illusion.

Instead, reality enfolds like the above-mentioned process of the caterpillar becoming a butterfly.

We too move from one state of reality to another while staying the same being.

The more conscious and present we can be in the dying process, the smoother it will be. The reason death has been labelled the *hour of reckoning* is based on the understanding that at the end of the dying process, perhaps life's most important initiation awaits us. It is there that we are confronted with the consequences of our actions from our last incarnation, and through these we gain insight into how we can magnify the frequencies of all-embracing presence, unconditional love and compassion the next time we incarnate. These are the qualities that characterize the Law of Light and thus the energies that govern our very being, the universe and all creation. When the God Consciousness in us is developed and refined, humans will no longer be trapped in their self-created limitations and will take a significant step up the ladder of spiritual evolution.

When my father was dying, I sat by his bedside. Every day, when my mum and I visited him, he asked me if I had bought a new car. I had just got separated after a long-term relationship and was driving a hire car at that time. I thought it was a strange worry to have when you're about to leave this world. Only later did I realize that the question was important to him because my father was a former taxi driver, and the car was the means of transport he was envisioning leaving this world in.

My father's hospitalization happened at a time when I had not had contact with Calle for almost six months. One day, as my mum and I were driving to the hospital, my phone rang. It was Calle:

"Yeah, hi there, I just wanted to let you know that today is the day your dad is leaving. Just so you can do what needs to be done. Bye."

Immediately I knew that I had to buy the car my father had so often asked about. Silkeborg is known as the "city of cars" with a sea of car dealerships that almost form a ring around the city, so I stopped at the first one and found a used car that matched my financial capabilities. Back at the hospital, I was able to reassure my father that I had bought a new car. He nodded in acknowledgement and it was clear that the message made him calm and relaxed.

After a while, he slipped into a sleep-like state while uttering incomprehensible sounds. When he came round a little later, he looked at me in surprise:

"Are you still here?"
"Yes," I replied. "Are you in pain?"
"No," he replied.

Another time when he came back to his outer awareness, he asked me if it was Svend Aage who was driving the car.

206

Svend Aage was his deceased older brother. This was repeated countless times until a young doctor asked me to follow him outside. There he announced that it was clear that my father was in severe pain and that they had to give him morphine. I told the doctor that my father didn't feel any pain and that he had refused morphine because he could not tolerate it. Nevertheless, as the nurse was believing that the sounds he was uttering were an expression of pain and restlessness, the doctor pressed me to allow them to implement the minimal dose. And so it was. After the morphine drip was applied, I had no more contact with my father, who "passed away quietly" an hour later.

Six months later, on a cold and dark winter evening, I was travelling south of Aarhus to give a lecture. As I passed the local racetrack, I saw out of the corner of my eye that lights were suddenly switched on at the track where my father had spent so much time. When I turned my face to see if it could be true, the lights went out again. This was repeated a few times until I suddenly felt my father's presence in the car. There was no doubt. It happened so fast. I remember trying to collect all the questions I had wanted to ask him as I was afraid he would quickly disappear again just like the lights on the racetrack.

"Don't worry, we have all the time we need," said his voice inside me.

During the half-hour it took me to drive to my destination, I had the most meaningful conversation with my father. The first thing he told me was that the morphine had made his transition to the other side more difficult. He wanted to share this information with me because it was essential knowledge for two women who had independently sought me out for help with their dying process.

"It's important to be as clear as possible during the transition," he said.

"If there is pain, and it's too severe, you will need a little help."

He then gently asked me to let go of my guilt and worry about my little sister, because:

"She is incarnated again, happily married, has children and a good life."

The last thing he said was this:

"And her flower up here is looking so beautiful."

He then showed me that we all have a so-called Soul Flower on a higher level of consciousness and that it is there, to this essence of our soul, that we are returning in between each incarnation, to "nourish" our precious flower with all the experiences we have had in the span of our past lifetime.

This was the purest contact I ever had with my father. It was his true being, free from any kind of noise, that came to me in my car that winter evening.

"There is a glorious pattern for every man's life, an individual, perfect pattern. No two people are alike ... No two leaves are alike – no two snowstorms – no two sets of fingerprints. No two lives are alike, yet each life holds a divine pattern of unfoldment, a great and holy destiny, rich in achievement and honor. As you live true to the pattern of yourself, that deep, inner self, you will unfold as perfect, as joyous, as naturally beautiful as the tree will reach its full measure of fulfillment." (Annalee Skarin)

17

THE GENEROUS HUMAN BEING

**"From tower to temple, from me to we,"
says the raindrop to the sea**

We have truly entered the Age of Aquarius. Time has come for us to transform the old paradigms: the race for social status, power, materialism, greed, cynicism, arrogance and indifference. It is therefore no longer about what we can get, but what we are able and allowing to give.

We are all, each of us, incarnated for a purpose. We are all expressions of a divine generosity, and it is this generosity that we have come here to share with others. To such an extent that there is no more room for the ego's little games, no more room for the tiring and in every way exhausting self-aggrandizement and narcissism, where inferiority and megalomania are always two sides of the same coin: a lack of understanding the unspeakable beauty of living in a caring and compassionate relationship to all that is, including one's own personality or inner child.

It's time to seek balance. To allow gratitude, joy and unconditional love and presence to flow freely through us. There is no doubt in my mind that we are all – on a personal and collective level – being confronted with our own shadows right now. And what a gift this is. Time has come to face old habits and unresolved topics about ourselves and the way we interact with others. Partly to revise the journey of this lifetime, but also to break old individual and collective patterns that are no longer serving us. And while the waves of the cosmic shift are getting stronger, it will become less and less tolerable or even possible for us to stay in the frequencies that once belonged to our personalities.

Our times are characterized by a rise of division and separation. During the recent and alleged Covid pandemic, we were encouraged not to visit our friends and family and have any physical contact with each other. As this basic element of experiencing human care and belonging was removed, it became much harder to accept alternative views and settle conflicts if someone had a different opinion to ourselves. In marriages, friendships and work relationships, we experienced disruption and division.

We all have opinions about everything and anything. This is especially evident on social media, where the tone is all too often irreconcilable. We get caught up in dramas we don't feel comfortable being a part of, we lose our balance and often end up in a cul-de-sac of locked options that ultimately only lead to frustration and unhappiness. We sometimes act rashly and react immaturely because we didn't take time to really listen or allow ourselves to think of that extra step that could have led to a more positive outcome. The old recipe of *counting to twenty* when you feel the rise of a disturbing emotion as well as the advice of *sleeping on* a matter before answering someone in a conflict situation cannot be remembered often enough.

We accuse each other of this or that, often forgetting to look at our own role in a conflict. Nothing is easier than pointing the finger at others. But what is "blaming others" but a veil over our own failures and mistakes? Yes, I feel betrayed, but maybe the betrayal materialized because I allowed it to happen. Perhaps I should have paid more attention and seen that it was my own vanity or fear that blinded me, so that I didn't react to the alarm bells that tried to warn me against continuing down a path I would normally have been aware would lead to nothing positive.

If only we would realize that the "enemy" is there to make us look at ourselves. When we fail to do this and subsequently miss this opportunity to change our beliefs or our behaviour, it is ourselves, our blindness or unwillingness (the real enemy) that will repeat similar situations – with different external "enemies", scenarios, locations and costumes, yet always around the same topic.

When we turn our backs on the painful but deeply liberating truth, we continue to project our own ills onto the people or circumstances around us: "It's so unfair that this job has not been offered to me!", "Why did my family do that to me?", "Why was I not born in a different place?", "It's everyone else that's wrong. I'm the innocent victim".

Any judgement of other people is an act of ignorance. In fact, we have no ground or means to judge anyone, as we cannot know why "others" act the way they do. I write "others" in quotation marks because in truth there are no "others", there is only US. Maybe you have also had an experience of an argument with someone, in which "you were right" – in your own perception, in the perception of your friends and family or even in the eyes of the law – but you cannot feel any happiness, because you know that the other person has not changed their opinion and now feels defeated or humiliated. The practice of blessing will help the other person and yourself. A constant stream of golden Light between your heart spaces will be established, that will allow both of you to transform the disharmonic field between you. Don't focus on *if, how or when* the relationship could change for the better again. Just keep streaming love and goodwill.

Another practice, if we are facing challenging relationships or situations in our lives, is to focus on gratitude instead of using our energy to assure, prove, discuss or convince someone. Start with feeling gratitude for all that you have ever received in life, big and small. The tension in your body, your heart and mind will immediately cease. It is very powerful and transformational to then express your gratitude to all those who went before you, who took care of you, who never focused on your faults but rather on the Light they saw you had hidden away in a corner of your heart. The vibration of your field will shift immediately once you let go of the carousel of painful thoughts and emotions. You will experience a feeling of belonging and community. And slowly but surely your relationships and personal living conditions will change, too.

We have the opportunity to make a difference in this day and age of orchestrated separation and enticed uniformed compliance, by stopping to resist the choices of others while allowing ourselves to stay anchored in the frequencies of Love, Peace, Gratitude and Blessing, no matter the circumstances. It is possible to live with each other without being either "for" or "against" anything. In truth, we all are TOGETHER aboard a ship that will either capsize or weather the storm that lies ahead. And although it may look like some of us are drilling holes in the ship's hull while others are desperately pouring water out of the sinking ship, in the end we have to come to terms with the fact that we are all in the same boat. If the ship goes down, we all go down with it. We cannot afford to belittle, ridicule or ignore the transformative power of living a life of peacefulness and goodwill. It is the cornerstone of all change, whether in our families, our communities, our political and economic spheres or in our spiritual connection with all life.

When we come to ourselves and realize that the distress, imbalances and conflicts that exist in the world are due to our choices, we also understand that it is possible to change our choices at any time. This is the opportunity and the power we have in every new moment. Now. What needs to change in our lives? What needs to change in society? Any change must always stem from a refined sharpening of our own awareness: why do I act the way I do? What are my innermost motives? Do I live up to my own inner calling and the ethical and spiritual principles with which I meet the world and my fellow human beings?

Personally, I believe that an important part of a necessary shift is to separate all forms of commercial economic interests from any kind of humanitarian, health-related, educational, legal and political mission. The various industries have no place in the councils and boards that exist solely to ensure the wellbeing of citizens. If we can start there, much can be changed for the better. The many recent scandals have shown that the forces that control money and political power are unscrupulous. It is always the strong that survive and set the agenda. Therefore, it is up to each of us to take responsibility for not increasing the distance and separation that has crept in everywhere, but instead to build bridges and face each other and the challenges. Regardless of the disagreements and differences that seem to separate us.

Whether you believe in the existence of the harmonious Consciousness of love, eternity and truth called God, or not – to me life is an expression of a unique form of divine generosity. A generosity that should be allowed to flow freely through us, so that it becomes a perceivable and accessible reality wherever we go. This means that, despite the noise that surrounds us, we too must always try to focus on the Light that shines in every human being we meet or think about, no matter how dim that Light may seem, no matter what thoughts or emotions they trigger in us. Through our focus, we can help to reflect the Light of another person, amplifying it instead of darkening or extinguishing it with an emotional or judgemental perception. We ourselves create a world of darkness or a world of Light with every thought or emotion we express. Remember the words of Yeshua. Do not hide your Light away but open your heart so that it can illuminate everything and everyone who comes near it.

NOW is the moment, when we can make a difference. No matter what or who is in front of us. Open your heart. And keep it open. Feel the field of power, peace and harmony all around you, waiting for you to recognize it. No need to protect your open heart, because once we allow the out-streaming of love, it will always flood through and transform any appearances and emotions. Open it softly and tenderly. Like the first blossom in spring. Listen. And trust. Open it wide in an instant, like a lightening force of joy that could make you shout from all rooftops. Follow its dance, its rhythm of care and kindness, tender and wild, let its music sound through your being to all corners of this world. Stay aware of your Light. Be still. Listen to it. Can you hear it? There it is. The music. I can hear it. It's here. It's here. Now. Sing, dance and let the rhythm of your heart and breath dissolve discouragement and hopelessness, fear and sadness, anger and pride, guilt and criticism, loneliness and judgement. Send your generosity, gratitude, healing and compassion out to humanity and the world. We need it. We need each other. Every single one of us.

Most people have heard of the Butterfly Effect. It's a theory that describes that a tiny change in some part of a system can cause a huge effect somewhere else: a butterfly, softly beating its wings on one side of the Earth, can trigger a hurricane on the other. The underlying wisdom behind this idea has its roots in Taoism. If we knew that everything we humans think, feel, say and do – and sometimes fail to do – affects the world in the same way as the beat of a butterfly's wings, we would be more conscious of our actions.

Unfortunately, the misconception that there is no God, no Divine Consciousness or afterlife has led many people to place little value on their attitudes or behaviour. Before we "do as we please", it is important to remember that each one of us is part of a whole. Everything created is a part of each other. Life is not only about ourselves and our immediate family, with other people being temporary extras in a private theatre play as long as they serve our interests and wellbeing.

Human Beings are not heartless or without compassion. If it sometimes seems that way, it's because a false perception of what the meaning of life is has crept in.

There are people who do not find it unconscionable to exploit others, who can steal and deceive without a care in the world. There are also people who, consciously or unconsciously, take on the role of victim in order to get what they want. In general, it has become commonplace for "the clever" to cheat the "less clever", which usually means that the unscrupulous take advantage of those who naturally trust others until proven otherwise.

There are also people who do not understand that the help they are trying to impose on others who have not asked for it or simply do not want any help or support may not come from pure motives. Just as the victim has made a habit of going through life appealing to the conscience and compassion of others, there are "human servants" who manipulate by always wanting to "do good". And when these mechanisms or strategies are revealed or rejected, this often results in anger and new emotional manipulations. For all these types of people, there is an agenda of hidden control of others that can be difficult to recognize.

Our times have produced a disturbing type of person with sociopathic and narcissistic traits that can be found in all walks of life but seems to feel most at home in high places where their manic charisma distorts and seduces the easily influenced who don't recognize the abuse of power until they are suddenly confronted with unexpected events, actions or constraints. Such people can also be found in religious and spiritual contexts. But wherever you find them, they can usually be spotted by the fruits of their enterprise. Make no mistake. Much "good" has been done by such people, but there is always a shadow over the outcome, a shadow that often means that the "good" done ultimately fails because there was a hidden or double-sided agenda behind it.

This is not a condemnation of people with personality disorders but an invitation to all of us to look deep within ourselves, because we too may carry hidden agendas that stem from unrecognized, selfish motives. Again and again, we must dare to ask ourselves what moves us to speak and act the way we do. What do we want to achieve?

The mystic, sage and one of the founding fathers of psychotherapy Carl Gustav Jung said that an inflated consciousness is always egocentric – conscious only of its own existence and nothing else. It is incapable of learning from past experiences, understanding current events or drawing correct conclusions about the future. It cannot be argued with, as it is experiencing a state of self-hypnosis. Spiritual practice is the way to encounter these seemingly unchangeable states in our personalities as well as in people or structures with whom we may be in conflict.

During national or global crises, an entire population can be hypnotized by charismatic leaders who know how to appeal to the lowest common denominator of their citizens, producing scenarios of fear and unrest, while appealing to the moral responsibility of the citizens and subsequently introducing solutions and new norms that before the crisis were considered completely unacceptable. It is far from the truth that the so-called "normal" is always in accordance with the Law of Light. We have an unreflected and unchallenged collection of beliefs that includes the conviction "if a majority says so, it must be right". But what if a collective anaesthesia or enchantment has crept into this majority, as the world experienced before, during and after the two great world wars? Such collective estrangement usually leads to total alienation from the individual's perception of themselves and the world around them and a severed connection to God Consciousness.

The American historian and civil rights activist Howard Zinn has repeatedly taken a critical look at the public debate on civil disobedience. In his opinion, the problem in the USA and the world today is not civil disobedience, but civil obedience. Obedience in the face of poverty, starvation, stupidity, war and cruelty. Obedience that allows the prisons to be filled with petty thieves while the grand thieves are running the country. Obedience to the warmongering dictates of politicians who, out of inhumanity and greed for power, cause the killing, impoverishment and injury of millions of citizens. As a former World War II pilot, he became an ardent opponent of war. Referring to a movie about the traumatic experience of an idealistic young soldier and his friends in the First World War, *All Quiet on the Western Front*, he often stressed that he considers it a crime to lure young men who are still kids to enrol into the army through any kind of propaganda about duty or national identity that glorified wars – as well as the men who volunteer to participate in them.

Will the rulers and the powerful ever value and treat the lives of young men and women as the precious treasures of divine heritage that they are? Will *we* ever stop allowing our leaders to use the sons and daughters of our human family as manipulable, controllable and strategic material and cannon fodder?

The great challenge for humans today is that we must dare to act from our own deepest conscience, even though it may point away from the crowd. Any reaction that is born out of fear creates dissonance with God Consciousness. Jewish psychologist Viktor E Frankl explains what compassion in action can do even under the most horrific circumstances in his deeply moving book *Man's Search for Meaning*, about his time as a prisoner in the Auschwitz concentration camp during World War II, where the war outside was reflected on a micro level in the struggle for survival between prisoners.

In the book, Frankl describes how prisoners who found the energy and compassion within to give what little they had to fellow prisoners closer to death than themselves were often the ones who survived the horrors, even if some of them died in the camp. Frankl writes about a certain blessedness that surrounded these prisoners, established through their acts of kindness, while those prisoners who disregarded any kind of care and dignity – and were completely devoid of compassion, were able to take the last dry piece of bread out of the mouth of a dying fellow prisoner, and even before he had drawn his last breath appropriated the dying man's shoes – usually became victims of their own hardening: being robbed of both bread and shoes, dignity and blessedness.

However, when a person over-emphasizes dignity and compassion, they cut themselves off from God Consciousness. Instead of resonance, dissonance is created. And dissonance weakens any kind of stamina and vigour. The opposite is true for those who have opened themselves to God Consciousness and therefore resonate in accordance with the Law of Light. From such a person you can sense an elevated energy level and sometimes see the ethereal radiance of gratitude, graciousness, generosity, kindness, presence and joy that stands like a halo around their whole being. This radiance activates hidden potential in the people such a person meets on their path, opening hearts and dissolving imbalances. Existence itself has become a living prayer.

Viktor Frankl's story is indisputable proof that God Consciousness is real, precisely because, regardless of external circumstances that could be perceived as impassable hermetically sealed gates, humans are able to open their hearts and connect with the highest principles of God Consciousness that continually expresses Itself to us – for example as compassion for a suffering fellow human being. Through his account we can begin to trust that it is *never* the circumstances that don't allow us to be kind or caring. It always is our own closed door in front of our heart, the hermetically sealed gate in modern humanity that can and must be opened. The survival of humanity depends on the success of a collective heart-opening process, and all of us are called to be both witnesses and facilitators on this amazing journey of awakening. As a means of support on the way, here is a quote from the German philosopher and, unbeknown to most, poet Friedrich Nietzsche:

"He who has a WHY to live for, can endure almost any HOW."

We certainly are living in such times of endurance. Manifold burdens are pressing on the hearts and shoulders of humanity. The question that modern mankind must ask itself is why we are here right now? Those who have misunderstood the wisdom of the East and believe that existence is an illusion and that our presence here is a mere coincidence that has no meaning, impact or consequence for ourselves or those around us, are in for a big surprise.

Yes, we are here to experience, to dance, create, heal, love, cry and laugh. But never at the expense of other people or other living beings. True selflessness is indeed a Self-filled-ness, a state in which we are connected with the eternal Harmonious in us, a state in which everything and everyone is considered, without any reference to gain or loss. Philosopher and historian Thomas Carlyle expresses this attitude of not demanding anything from others, from life or from nature in his own uncompromising way:

> "Brother! The brave man must give his life away. Give it, I advise you – you don't expect to be able to sell it satisfactorily, do you? Give it away like a royal heart, and let the price be nothing. In this way you will get everything for it. The heroic – and isn't every human being, thanks to God, a potential hero? – will have to act like this, at all times and in all circumstances."

Every form of life that unfolds in the universe is divine. The wise and compassionate destroy nothing, hurt no one and protect the inherent right of every living being to fulfil its destiny. We kill small lives with every thoughtless step and larger lives with every thoughtless word. There is no such thing as thoughtlessness that causes no pain to anyone or anything. When we love life, it's easy to be thoughtful: but when we don't care or we consider ourselves unfairly treated, we are less thoughtful. The pain we cause returns to us, and we must be ready to account for our careless inconsideration at any time.

May the Taoist master Chuang Tzu close this chapter:

"He in whom the Tao unfolds without hindrance,
does not harm other beings with his actions.
Yet he does not experience himself
as being 'good' or 'caring'.
The one in whom Tao unfolds without hindrance,
is not preoccupied with his own interests
and does not look down on others who are.
He makes no effort to earn money
and makes no virtue of being poor.
He goes his own way without leaning on others
and does not make it a point to walk alone.
Even if he doesn't follow the herd himself,
he does not complain about those who do.
Rank and reward do not tempt him;
dishonour and shame do not deter him.
He is not always looking for right and wrong
always concerned with 'Yes' or 'No'.
Hence the ancients of old said:
'The man of Tao remains unknown.
"No self" is the "true Self".
And the greatest man is nobody.'"

18

PRACTICE

We are family in eternity

Healing dance with the Ether

A powerful tool for healing or reaching a state of peace is to infuse energy from the ether that surrounds us into our energetic field and every cell of our physical body. You are standing with your legs slightly apart. Be soft in the knees so that you are standing in a secure yet mobile way on the ground. Feel your connection with Mother Earth, her welcome, her nurturing energy streaming through the soles of your feet into your whole body. Open your chest, open your heart. Let its Light stream out into all directions, as far as you wish: toward the space in front of you, behind you, to your right, to your left, to the space above you as well as below you. Slowly sway back and forth, side to side, as you caress the ether with your hands and let them dance tenderly with its fabric of beauty. Open the palms of your hands and open your fingertips to the contact with the life force of the ether. Allow yourself to merge with this field of completion and harmony. At some point, when you clearly feel the presence and pulsations of the ether, direct the energy with your hands to the organ that needs healing. If you want to release an emotion, feel where the tension of that emotion has manifested in your body and stream the area with etheric life force. Stay aware of your breath. Give up all control. Enjoy the waves of being breathed in and out. Be present in every movement you make. Be free. Forget about how you look. Give yourself to the moment. To the dance. And *be* it.

Ouroboros meditation

The Fire is in the Wind
The Wind is in the Tree
The Tree is in the Rain
The Rain is in the Cloud
The Cloud is in the Sky
The Sky is in Man
Man is in the Atonement
The Atonement is in God
God is in the Silence
The Silence is in the Heart
The Heart is in the Fire

Fire is a metaphor for creation and for purification. Yochanan the Baptist said: "I baptise you with water, but after me comes one who will baptise you with fire and the Holy Spirit." *Fire* is the transforming and cleansing power here, while *the Wind* is the omnipresent Holy Spirit.

The Wind in the Tree indicates that the Holy Spirit is everywhere. *The Tree* stands for our access to wisdom, calmness and memory.

The Rain stands for emotional cleansing, for the transformation of emotions. Tears are shed in joy and in sorrow.

The Cloud symbolizes any transient phenomenon, any transformation. *The Cloud* is another state of water, just like fog, snow and ice. These changing states become one in *Heaven*, which is the Heaven Yeshua says is within us.

The Sky is the all-harmonious expression of Divine Consciousness, and it is present *in Man* (in all humans) as an active frequency of individualized God Consciousness.

The Atonement expresses our ever-present possibility of changing a perceived wrong or injury through gaining an understanding of the cause of consequences we are facing. The always available opportunity to re-evaluate thoughts, words and actions. When we consciously accept responsibility for all that we have done and continue to do, an inner transformation is being initiated, which is necessary in our endeavour to become one with *God Consciousness*. The English term *Atonement* reveals the essence of its meaning better than any other language. When the transformation is successful, *Atonement* becomes At-one-ment, unity with *God*.

God is omnipresent, but it is *in the Silence* that we most effectively unite with *God Consciousness*. *The Silence* of the heart is the place in us from which we can most purely fulfil our purpose. When we allow our thoughts and words to pass through the filter of the heart before we manifest them through action in the physical world, we are in accordance with the Law of Light.

The Heart in the Fire tells of the purification that is going on all the time, through everything we do. When we practise the Ouroboros Meditation, we automatically polish the mirror of the Heart so that we will be able to be the clear and pure reflectors of God Consciousness, expressing it in a peaceful, open, caring, joyful, loving and compassionate attitude.

Thus, the Ouroboros Meditation expresses the eternal cycle of life and our true place and purpose in creation.

Home in *Rukha*

Since *Rukha (Spirit)* and *Rukha d'Koodsha (Holy Spirit)* dissolve and transform all errors or transgressions of the Law of Light, *Rukha* is the key ingredient in any forgiveness process. When we forgive another human being, it is not the other person's "offence" that we are now changing through our seemingly selfless act. We are consciously ceasing to continue our pain- and reproach-filled reactive attitude toward the other person and stop the ongoing recreation of the particular event in our mind.

Forgiveness in Aramaic, *shbag,* means to erase, to transform. If we want to forgive, we need to erase any judgement we may have toward the person we believe has offended us. We transform our outrage, frustration, anger, resentment, sadness into a peaceful state by entering into our innate Consciousness of the All-Harmonious beyond any duality. Instead of holding on to "the culprit" by focusing on "the offence", and even sharing our emotions and thoughts with others, we can start a good rumour that focuses on his or her positive qualities. We take responsibility for ourselves and allow others to do the same. This is how dark matter is transformed into Light and unconditional love, *Rakhma,* is manifested wherever we go.

1. Sit with a straight back in a relaxed state of presence. Allow your body to be totally relaxed. Go through your body part by part to become aware of any tensions. Give these the time and attention you need to allow the tension to dissolve. Once this is accomplished, gather your whole being into the practice you are about to begin.
2. Pay attention to your breath. Open your chest by straightening up and pulling your shoulders down and slightly back. Feel completely open and aligned in your spine and connected to the etheric field around you.
3. Breathe in deeply, allowing your lungs and stomach to expand. Hold your breath for a moment and exhale while pulling your stomach inward. This is done without effort. It is important not to hyperventilate.
4. Visualize that you are breathing in through the Heart. Breathe in from all directions, toward the centre of the heart, while thinking *Ruuuuuuuu* on the inhalation and

saying *khaaaaaaa* aloud on the exhalation. Make sure you breathe as deeply and slowly as possible. Inhale: stomach out – exhale: stomach in.

5. As you immerse yourself in this practice, notice how with each breath you awaken the God Consciousness within you. Allow this awareness to permeate your entire body, every organ, every cell and all layers of your being. You ARE God Consciousness. You are a living, pulsating field of eternal all-harmonious Consciousness. It is your one true reality, beyond all experiences in duality. Now you know what true gratitude is and what it feels like.

If you want to expand this practice, you can do so by using the mantra *Rukha d'Koodsha* (Holy Spirit) on the inhale and *Malkoota d'Shmeya* (Kingdom of Heaven) on the exhale.

This is my favourite practice and I have done it for many years. It has helped me many a time to dissolve stagnated and critical situations. I practise it everywhere: in the supermarket, on the train, at the kitchen sink, in lectures and workshops, in large gatherings and in one-to-one conversations. This prayer produces, for me, the highest level of presence. And most importantly, it keeps me awake and present so that I don't forget why I'm here.

Blessing

The practice of blessing is a most powerful tool for healing and transformation. Give yourself a timeframe, for example a week, so you can see the change in you and in your relationships.

Most people feel a shift very quickly, often even right from the moment of decision. Wherever you are, whomever you meet, surround them with a golden sphere of the most beautiful and powerful Light, so everyone in the street, the train, the supermarket, the theatre, the school, the office, the hospital, the children's playground, the gym, the restaurant, the airport, the car – your family, friends and colleagues, neighbours or strangers – all of them will be walking, talking, sitting, sleeping in these beautifully beaming and radiating hubs of golden Light and life force. Give the Light the quality you feel like sharing, may it be joy, peace, grace, ease, healing, love ... Find your own words, that you, in your heart, silently speak to them, for example: "I bless you! May you walk well and happy through this beautiful day!" Or: "I bless you! My heart greets yours, I love you! May everything you wish for come true!" Or: "I bless You! My Dear Brother/Sister in the Light! May you feel guided and loved wherever you go!" Or: "I bless You! So much Gratitude and Love to you!"

As we continue to *bestow* a blessing on everyone we meet (including ourselves), all day long, come rain or shine, we will feel a major shift in our awareness. Maybe we want to give ourselves completely to the practice – and *become* a blessing. Remembering in the morning, just after waking up, that we *are* a blessing. Dedicating ourselves to connect with this truth throughout our day – for example every full hour. Be still and take a moment to feel your field beyond your body. You are a pulsating, radiating and distributing Being of love, magnificence and joy, sharing all of your Light with everyone, with no exception and no expectation! The sun shines on everyone. So do we. Imagine a field of sunflowers. Every morning the sunflowers are awakened by and open toward the sun. All day through they are blessed by its warm nourishing beams of light and follow its path across the sky. We can be that sun. Our open, overflowing heart is all we need when we rise in the morning and begin a new day. Now we *are* the quality, the frequency that we wish to receive! Whatever we want to see in the world, it is up to us to provide and anchor the much-needed vibrational consciousness – with might and dedication, no matter what other people do or do not do.

When we *bestow* a blessing by sending a thought of good will and our love and compassion toward someone, it is a horizontal deed, while the *becoming* adds a vertical dimension to the blessing that not only transforms any dispute or error but ignites the Light in us – and consequently in and around everybody we meet.

Both the receiver as well as the sender are being raised toward the frequency of the *equal-armed cross* of blessing, in which they will have access to their *napsha*, the essence of their soul. We radiate out blessings to others while we dwell in a golden sphere of Light, fully connected to our Light Body. Being in this world but not from this world. Blessing everyone, friends or foes. Not searching for a way but *being* the way.

Do not forget to include your ancestors as well as your Guardian Angel and your Spirit Guides into your day of ceaseless blessing. You will receive the most beautiful and powerful strings of golden Light in return.

Another powerful practice of Blessing is to silently share the activated presence of the Holy Spirit and the Kingdom of Heaven (see practice *Home in Rukha* above) with those we meet.

Inhale *Rukha d'Koodsha* (Holy Spirit) through your heart chakra in the middle of the breastbone and exhale *Malkoota d'Shmeya* (Kingdom of Heaven) into the heart of the other, over and over.

We can do this practice even without having a person in front of us. In this case, we are streaming out the frequency of *Rukha d'Koodsha – Malkoota d'Shmeya* into the space around us, wherever we are. Day and night. While walking the streets, going to the supermarket, doing domestic work, talking to people, writing emails, making love. It will slowly but surely turn our inside out, so that the blessing within will become the blessing that we are and with which we meet all living beings.

Healing butterfly hands

Visualize and feel your breath and the life force from the ether streaming into your heart, arriving from all directions while thinking *Ruuuuuuuu* and then breathing out through the centre of the palms of your hands on *khaaaaa*. Feel how the centre of the palms become more and more charged in this way until they pulse with energy. When you feel the energy flowing freely, let your hands float like butterflies over the client's body at a distance of about 5–10 centimetres (2–4 inches) from the body, transferring the energy to the places that need healing *Rukha* energy. Visualize and feel gas-blue Light radiating from the centre of your palms for some moments, and then allow golden Light to flood through them. To conclude the healing, use Yeshua's blessing, *Ikhal – Be blessed and protected.*

Travelling the ether

Agree with a friend or partner to do the following exercise.

You are each in a different location. It can be in the same city or you can be, for example, in New York while your friend is in London. Agree in advance which of you will be the sender and which will be the receiver, and arrange an appointed time for and length of the practice.

For the outreaching sender:

1. You are sitting on a chair. Start with the *Rukha* practice as described above.
2. Who are you and what do you want to achieve? Quietly say your name, what you want to achieve with the upcoming journey and why you are doing it: "I am (name). I want to find the cause of the suffering of my friend (name) and I want to be a channel for his/her healing after I have received the information".

3. Close your eyes and visualize yourself travelling the distance between New York and London (or wherever you both happen to be) to the address where your friend is located, and you will be there in an instant.
4. Visualize where in the flat or room your friend is. Is he or she lying or sitting?
5. Once you have a clear sense of your friend, feel and investigate the whole field around him or her and use your butterfly hands to scan your friend's Light Body, which is 5–10 centimetres (2–4 inches) out from his or her physical body. When you find the spot on the body where your friend needs attention or healing, let your hand hover over that spot while silently reciting the command: *Ephatah! Be opened!* Visualize gently placing your hand on the exposed spot on the physical body, revitalizing the weak Light particles by sending gas-blue Light from the palm of your hand into the area, followed by golden Light.
6. Finish with the blessing *Ikhal! – Be blessed and protected!*
7. Withdraw quietly and travel home.

The receiving person sits or lies down and relaxes completely for the entire time agreed upon.

When the practice is completed, communicate with each other.

The receiver first tells what he/she experienced during the healing. The healer shares his/her experience of the meeting afterwards. You can switch roles the next day to practise your ability to work in the ether. Keep a diary of your practices, especially if you are working with different people. In that way you can keep track of your experiences and challenges along the way.

The Heavenly Prayer

Heavenly Source of all Being
You who are everywhere
Blessed be Your Holy Vibration.
Fill us with Your Grace
Here and now and for evermore.
Open our hearts and minds to Your Consciousness
And release us from the fetters
With which we bind ourselves and each other.
Lead us into the Presence of Your Light
And let us rest in our Higher Self
Until we are at one with You.
We come with Joy and Compassion
To unite with the Essence of the Love that we are.
May this holy moment be the ground
From which our future actions grow.
Amen.

Heavenly Source of all Being

"Heavenly Source of all Being" equals "God" or pure Consciousness. Humans are born in the image of God, which means that we are individualized God Consciousness and have the ability to express all divine qualities. We are vibrational beings. Through the prayer we recognize our relationship with the origin and reality of all life, God Consciousness, and connect with its presence and frequency.

You who are everywhere

God Consciousness is everywhere. As Yeshua says in the *Gospel of Thomas*: "Split the tree and lift the stone, and God (I AM) is there." God is the life-giving principle and power in everything, not just in this universe, but in all universes. "My Father's Kingdom has many mansions". When we see ourselves and other people through the God Consciousness within us, we see the true essence of all living beings.

Blessed be Your Holy Vibration

Traditionally translated as "Blessed be Thy Name". The Aramaic word for *Name* stems from the root word *SHM*, which also means *Vibration, Light /Consciousness, Sound, the Image of God in all humans*. With this line, we recognize and bless the thread of life that connects all creation to each other. We are ONE, and we are ONE with God, the All-Harmonious Consciousness and Vibration. This relationship can never not be. It is only when we fall into selfishness that we momentarily turn our backs to it and consequently cannot perceive it anymore.

Fill us with Your Grace, here and now and for evermore

This is the invocation of God Consciousness – that it may be realized in our lives on all levels. If we "fall", we understand why it happened, and find the strength to get up again. We realize that our personalities can be right or wrong, and many phases in our life have a beginning and an end while at the same time God Consciousness is present in us, with us, through us and around us as the only reality that is true and eternal.

Open our hearts and minds to Your Consciousness and release us from the fetters with which we bind ourselves and each other

We humans enter into many different relationships. If we don't yet realize who we truly are and need recognition and attention, we bind ourselves to others in a way that is not in accordance with the truth of our being. We invent "debts" to bind other people to us: "If you help me, I help you". "If you agree with me, I agree with you". "If you love me, I love you". It's conditional love, instead of unconditional love. Unconditional love, *Rakhma*, gives without expecting anything in return. It sees where help is needed and steps in or passes by if it is not needed. This kind of love is free and manifests freedom everywhere it goes.

Lead us into the Presence of Your Light and let us rest in our Higher Self until we are at one with You

We are surrounded by many distractions that want our attention and keep us far away from perceiving the reality of harmony. But the biggest distractor is our own personality with its colourful portfolio of thoughts, beliefs, opinions, habits and emotions. Now we ask for help to think, speak and act from our Higher Self so we can live our everyday life in union with the God Consciousness within us. We surrender. We don't give up, but we GIVE IT UP – up to the highest frequency in our being.

We come with Joy and Compassion to unite with the Essence of the Love that we are

When we are sad and depressed because we feel hurt or lonesome, there is only one cure: to see it as a passing emotion we don't have to hang on to. Every emotion can shift from moment to moment. But we don't have to wait for the shift, we can choose to be joyful and compassionate here and now. By reciting this line, we instantly activate its frequency and become Joy and Compassion.

May this holy moment be the ground from which our future actions grow

Every moment is sacred in itself, but it is our ability to be empathetic, present and compassionate that makes this particular moment special. The mistakes we've made in the past can only be corrected by changing our behaviour NOW, and NOW, and NOW, and NOW. This is how we set ourselves and each other free.

You can repeat this prayer several times. It will calibrate your entire being and you will find the peace you need to sit in the silence described above. Your personal voice is calmed and you can now sit in the silence and listen. This is a sure way to contact the World of Answers. Sometimes the answers to your questions may not come immediately but appear at a later time via the events that human life offers. Through the *Heavenly Prayer*, we rise above the dramas of everyday life and realize the simple truth that we are all ONE.

Compassion is the Greatest Power

Reconciliation instead of punishment
Challenge instead of norm
Compassion instead of cynicism
Presence instead of distance
Humour instead of sarcasm
Organic instead of mechanical
Dynamic instead of static
Universal instead of national
Generosity instead of greed
Altruism instead of selfishness
Enlightenment instead of escapism
Awareness instead of numbing
Co-operation instead of competition
Wisdom of the heart instead of artificial intelligence
Clear and loving instead of cold and cynical.

When my mother, Alice Muhl, was laid to rest at the age of 94 in 2020, the burial coffee and cake was served in the village hall after the funeral ceremony. My mother was well known and respected in the village, so some people wanted to pay tribute to her by telling little anecdotes about her. It was very strange for me, who was very connected to her all my life, to suddenly gain insight into aspects of my mother's life that I had never known before.

One younger woman told me that one day she had had an important meeting and needed a nanny to look after her five-year-old child. The problem was that the child had never been looked after before, because he was always screaming and became very wild and frantic when he was alone with people he did not know well. My mum had obviously seen the mother and son before and knew about his behaviour with other people, but exclaimed without hesitation: "You just go, and I'll look after your boy."

And so it was. When the woman returned a few hours later, she couldn't believe her eyes or ears. The child was smiling and playing, completely calm, and everything seemed to be in harmony.

"But how is that possible?" the woman exclaimed. "What have you done to make him like that?"

To which my mum replied: "Oh, I just put a finger on his forehead and everything was fine."

This story prompted another woman to share her version of a similar incident. She had witnessed how my mum had calmed a distressed and barking dog tied up outside the local supermarket by similarly putting her index finger on its forehead. Instantly, it was silent and calm until its owner picked it up.

My mum apparently practised her own form of hands-on – or rather finger-on – healing in her daily environment without feeling compelled to share it with me. She didn't need to make a big deal of it, it was just something she did quietly when it was needed.

After Alice's death, a neighbour gave me a note from my mother. She had found it hidden away in the back of a drawer in a small telephone table, which the neighbour had saved from being taken to the dump. On the note was written in my mum's characteristic scrawl:

"Give each other love – don't be selfish.
Think of others and all fear will disappear."

19

ARAMAIC CORNERSTONES

Near or far – be the love that you are

CREATION
John 1:1–5

> "In the beginning was the Word, and the Word was with God, and the Word was God."

This is the cryptic opening to the *Gospel of John*, which has been the subject of much speculation and theological interpretation.

What is "the Word" referred to? The Word in Aramaic is pronounced *mila*, but the Aramaic *Gospel of John* reads *milta*, which means act of will, wilful action, command, directed display of power. Perhaps the translation of John 1:1–5 should read like this instead:

> "In the beginning *(brashet)* a willed power came into being *(milta),* and this power was with God, and God was this willed unfolding power *(milta)*. The beginning *(brashest)* came into being by the will of God. Everything was created by God and nothing was manifested except that which was destined. From God emanated perfect life *(khayi)* and this perfect life *(khayi)* became the

Light *(noohra)* that dissolved the darkness *(khishuka)* and enlightened man."

Brashet = To set a point from which everything new unfolds, as when one puts a pen to paper and from this point either writes a word, a sentence, a poem, or draws a line indicating a course, a life, a course of life, a continuous circle, a horizon or an upward or downward vertical line. The point is the present moment in which a new beginning unfolds. When we are aware of our own inner creative power, we know that every point we set is part of the eternal now that is pregnant with something new. Every moment offers a new beginning.

Khayi = Life, life force, true life, perfect life.

Noohra = Light, illuminated, enlightenment. Aramaic distinguishes between Light and darkness in the same way it distinguishes between insight and ignorance.

Khishuka = Darkness, ignorance.

DREAMS AND VISIONS
Numbers 12:6

"Dream" in Aramaic is *helma*. It derives from the root word *HLM,* "to dream". *HLM* also means "to heal, to make whole, to restore the fallen, to do good, to restore the original, divine state". The messages the Essenes and Therapists received in dreams were considered to be divine guidance, visions and prophecies. In a verse from Numbers 12:6, the Lord says to his prophets:

> "Hear my word *(mila)!* If you are true *(pshetta)* prophets, then I will make myself known to you in a vision *(helmi)* and I will speak to you in a dream *(helma)."*

When we understand the symbolic language that our nightly dreams are spun from, we have an ancient tool that is an important part of understanding who we are, where we come from and what our task is in the current incarnation. Dreams guide us and bring clarity to our understanding of the processes we are in the midst of and that we go through throughout our lives.

THE TRANSFORMATION OF THE EGO
Matthew 4:1–10

> "Then Yeshua was led by the spirit *(rukha d'koodsha)* into the wilderness *(madbra)* to be tempted *(naseh)* by the devil *(satana)*. After fasting for forty days and forty nights, he finally felt hunger. And the Tempter came and said to him, 'If you are the Son of God, tell these stones to become bread.' But in reply he said, 'It is written, "Man does not attain perfect life *(khayi)* by bread alone, but by every word *(mila)* that comes from the mouth of God". Then the devil took him into the holy city, and he placed him on the pinnacle of the temple and said to him, 'If you are the Son of God, throw yourself down, for it is written, 'He will command his Angels *(malakhi)* concerning you, and they will carry you in their hands, so that you will not strike your foot against any stone.'"

The rest of the passage relates how Yeshua is offered world dominion if only he will submit to the commands of the devil *(akelqazar, satana)*, to which Yeshua replies, "Get behind me, satan *(satana)*, for it is written that you shall honour God and God alone."

Madbra = Desert or wilderness; an unprotected inner state. During their practice of forty days of fasting, the Essenes dissolved the mental and emotional filter and shield with which we relate to the world. The desert or wilderness is thus a metaphor for the great, wide-open void or nothingness in which there is nothing left to hide behind or protect yourself with. You are existentially undressed and stand completely naked with nowhere to go – so that God can now find you. This state is the prerequisite for anchoring the awareness that you are a child of God.

Naseh = to be tempted, to be weighed, to test, to be tried, to face yourself and your fears. *Akelqazar, satana = The devil;* the tempter; the accuser; the adversary, which is equal to Yeshua's personal ego, which, after forty days of fasting, is becoming worried and ready to give up. The ego realizes that this process means its dissolution if the practice is completed. However, Yeshua has allied himself with the Holy Spirit *(Rukha d'Koodsha)* and through this union he resists the ego's attack and completes the initiation, strengthened for the mission that awaits him. This built the integrity that allowed Yeshua to fulfil his life purpose.

THE WAY WE SEE
Matthew 6:22–23

"The eye is the lamp of the body, therefore if your eye sees clearly *(pshetta),* your whole being will be illuminated *(noher),* but if your eye is dim *(bisha),* your whole being will be dark *(khishooka).* If the Light *(noohra)* that is in you is shrouded in darkness *(khishooka),* how extensive is this darkness *(khishooka)!*"

Pshetta = True, without fault, clear.
Noher = Enlightened.
Bisha = Evil, unclear, unbalanced, immature, sick, rotten, judgemental, scheming.
Noohra = Light.
Khishooka = Absence of Light, ignorance, darkness, mental imbalance.

The way you see and perceive is what determines if there is Light in your life. When you see and perceive without judgement, your whole being will be illuminated. When your perception is tainted and judgemental, your being will be darkened. How much darkness do you want to be surrounded with? How much Light do you want to be surrounded with?

THE BEATITUDES
Matthew 5:3–11

1 "A heavenly attitude is theirs *(touveyhoun)*, **whose home is in** *Rukha* **(Spirit); theirs is a heavenly/transpersonal state** *(Malkoota d'Shmeya)*

Touveyhoun = To be blessed, happy and content, peaceful and in an uplifted state; ripe; the perfect moment; the open Heart; exalted dignity, giving rise to thoughts and actions that are in harmony with the Heavenly Source of all creation.
Rukha (d'Koodsha) = The Holy Spirit, the part of the creative force that transforms all effects of error.
Malkoota d'Shmeya = The Kingdom of Heaven; a transpersonal state above and beyond the physical, emotional and mental personality; a universal attribute that sees humanity as a whole whose goal is to express good.

2 "A heavenly attitude is theirs, those who are conscious of their faults *(abilii)*; **they shall be cured of their mental stress** *(nitbeyoun)."*

Abilii = an awareness of wrongdoing that activates regret; sorrow; longing for truth; willingness to correct mistakes.
Nitbeyoun = Transforming grief over mistakes by facing them and taking responsibility for them; a form of rebirth through the relief of mental stress.

3 "A heavenly attitude is theirs, those with humility *(makikhii)*; they will win *(nartoun)* the Earth."

Makikhii = Humble; reverent; accommodating; peaceful; yielding.
Nartoun = To gain; to inherit; to deserve.

4 "A heavenly attitude is theirs, those who hunger for justice and truth *(kenoota)*; they shall attain it."

Kenoota = Sound; proper; right; just; righteous; honourable; true; honest; reasonable; real; a structure of mind that pervades right behaviour, that always seeks harmony with others, that does not take advantage of the weakness of others but seeks at every opportunity to remedy problems. Those who open themselves to this wisdom of the Heart and are absorbed by it, adopt an exalted attitude leading to the ultimate, harmonious God Consciousness.

5 "A heavenly attitude is theirs; those, whose love is without condition *(rakhmanii)*; they will, therefore, receive unconditional love *(rakhma)*."

Rakhma = The love and foundation on which the Law of Light rests; the love that is unconditional and makes no demands to be loved, rewarded or receive anything in return; pure love that involves a deep understanding of the essence of another human being.

6 "A heavenly attitude is the pure *(dadcean)* of Heart *(b'libhoun)*; they will see *(nikhazoun)* the Heavenly Source *(Alaha)*."

Dadcean = Without fault; trustworthy.
B'libhoun = To think with the Heart.

Nikhazoun = Seeing and understanding from a higher plane; the overview that sees the whole.

Alaha = The Consciousness behind all creation; the highest, most ultimate source of truth; the Heavenly Source.

7 "A heavenly attitude is theirs, those who serve *(abdey)* the peace of the Creator *(Shlama)*; they will be called the heirs of the Source."

Abdey = Effectively serving an exalted purpose, doing good through service.

Shlama = The peace that is beyond the world and is in accordance with the highest principles expressed in the Sermon on the Mount.

To surrender, to lay down one's arms, to drop one's masks and lower one's guard. A heavenly attitude is theirs, for whom true service is the only reality; they are at home with the Heavenly Source. Exalted are they in whom peace is the only guiding principle; they rest in the bosom of the Almighty.

8 "A heavenly and blessed attitude is theirs, those who are mocked and tormented *(radpean)*, against whom evil is spoken *(b'dagaloota)* because of their work for justice and right behaviour; theirs is a perfect inner peace and clarification *(Malkoota d'Shmeya)*."

Radpean = To mock in the sense of undermining and belittling.

B'dagaloota = A mind out of balance that must lie in order to be, which is false and treacherous in thought, speech and action.

Malkoota d'Shmeya = The Kingdom of Heaven. Here it is an attitude of balance, clarity and forgiveness in relation to the situation of being mocked or attacked.

The balanced and heavenly minded individual cannot be shaken by any subversive activity because such a person refuses to take any form of hostility and attack personally. Instead, scorn is transformed into understanding that embraces the scorner. Blessed is the one who, in the struggle for justice, despite the condemnation of others, is able to accommodate those who condemn them. Such a person occupies the heavenly position.

CONCLUSION

**The wisdom of your heart
knew it from the start**

Although the Beatitudes explained in Chapter 19 are 2,000 years old, they are more relevant than ever.

We live in an age where everyone wants to get ahead, has no patience, is unable to empathize with other people's situations and therefore often takes their wellbeing for granted. It is when we rush and let our emotions get the better of us that we should stop and examine ourselves and ask how we have ended up in a life wasted on chores that have nothing to do with our soul's purpose.

Such a condition can be cured. Hold back, let others join in and feel the joy of having made a situation easier for a fellow human being. Pick up what others drop. Be present and on the cutting edge instead of blind and numb. Be grateful when you can help someone who needs your help. Be grateful when another person sees you when you need help. How hard is that?

We shouldn't get carried away when we read a sensational headline in the newspaper without familiarizing ourselves with its background. We've become accustomed to the media delivering the truth, while the agenda is more about tantalizing our senses (hence the term sensa-tion) to get the most clicks. By allowing our nervous system to be flooded with this kind of noise again and again, we end up drowning in emotions that we must constantly seek to release in order to survive. This is done through shrill social media posts that are currently acting as a kind of electronic, mental-relief rubbish bin for people who seem to have completely forgotten what wonderful beings they really are. We cannot change the world by condemning others, only by changing our own behaviour.

Instead of passing on gossip, we can start a good rumour. That is, emphasize another person's qualities instead of focusing on the weaknesses that we all deal with. Why do something to others that would destroy ourselves if done to us?

We all have to leave here at some point. And even if we try to suppress this unwelcome fact, we can't outrun it. Consider children and the way they react. A child picks up on any emotional or mental energy. It is a commendable attitude when parents agree not to talk about problems while their child is overhearing the conversation. However, it is important to realize that most children are able to sense the energies present in their environment and therefore also react to unexpressed thoughts and feelings. As adults, we must learn to master our emotions so that we do not abuse our power, influence and position of trust to manipulate our children and teach them not to trust their own perceptions. We must also ensure we do not allow our emotions to cloud our own clarity – which we so desperately need to transform a world that has decided that peace can only be achieved through war. We don't need more half-hearted actionism, empty promises or well-meaning advice that is not grounded in experiential wisdom. We need authenticity and integrity and the courage to live Yeshua's words.

FAREWELL

**When all the talk is done,
all ways melt into One**

Sisters and Brothers, Fathers and Mothers,
Children of the Sky! It's time to ally.

In Grace we raise.
And walk these lands, as family, as friends.
We are here, together as One.
And it's clear – the old ways are done.
We serve each other, one hand and one heart.
No pain or bother can keep us apart.
No language, no border – Love is our order.

We sing our songs and right the wrongs.
We raise with might the dark into Light.
We are family in eternity.

We know why we came: We'll change this game.
Without shame, without blame.
It's on us to decide –
And we choose the Light.

Naleea

ABOUT THE AUTHORS

Lars Muhl is a Danish mystic, author and musician known for his exploration of spiritual topics, including Yeshua (Jesus), Mary Magdalene and the wisdom of the Essenes. From a young age, he has dedicated himself to the study of Aramaic, esoteric Christianity and world religions. His books have been translated into 10 languages and published in 27 countries.

Naleea Landmann is a German mystic, author, musician and actress. A natural-born intuitive, she has been collaborating and co-writing with Lars since 2017, working together in talks, workshops, concerts and on *The Light Within a Human Heart*, *The Sacred Numbers of Initiation* and *The God Formula*, which she translated into German.

Since early childhood, Naleea had a strong yearning to connect with the Divine and understand the realities of this world and the universe. Her out-of-body experiences led her to question "reality" already as a young child – her personal experiences as well as our path as humanity. Finding a way to express what she perceived and felt, she started to use acting as a tool to communicate and share light frequencies and healing energies of love and devotion, as well as an opportunity to understand the ways of our personality structures. Her vision is to live within a world of heart-centered beings, who listen to their own guidance and share themselves and their gifts in joy, true connection and Divine communion.

In 2023, she made her solo debut with the book *The Love That You Are – Psalm 119 Meditations*, a spiritual companion and guide to enter into the I AM Presence through prayer. The paraphrase on the 22 prayers from the Old Testament is available in English, German and Danish.

Stay updated on Lars' and Naleea's schedule of online classes, concerts and workshops by subscribing to their newsletter at Larsmuhl.com

BOOKS BY LARS MUHL

In English

The ⊙ Manuscript (*The Seer, The Magdalene, The Grail*), Lemuel Books, 2008
The ⊙ Manuscript (*The Seer, The Magdalene, The Grail*), Watkins, 2013
The Law of Light, Watkins, 2014
The Seer, Watkins, 2012, 2016
The Magdalene, Watkins, 2017
The Grail, Watkins, 2017
The Gate of Light, Watkins, 2018
The God Formula, Sacred Seed, 2020
The Wisdom of a Broken Heart, Watkins, 2021
The Light Within a Human Heart, Watkins, 2022
The Sacred Numbers of Initiation, Watkins, 2023
The True and The Eternal, Watkins, 2025 (with Naleea Landmann)

In German

Die Vergessene Sprache, Flensburger Hefte Verlag, 2011
Der Seher, Kamphausen, 2016
Der Magdalena, Kamphausen, 2017
Der Gral, Kamphausen, 2018
Die Gottes-Formel, Sacred Seed, 2020
Das Licht Im Herzen Der Menschen, Kamphausen, 2023

In French

Le Chercheur, Flammarion, 2017, 2018
Le Recontre, Flammarion, 2018, 2019
L'Union, Flammarion, 2019, 2020
Ө Manuscrit, Flammarion, 2020
La Vraie Formule De Dieu, Guy Trédaniel, 2021

In Dutch

De Ziener, Edicola, 2016, 2017, 2018, 2019
De Magdaleen, Edicola, 2016
De Graal, Edicola, 2017
Taxo Luma, Edicola, 2020
Reis Naar Je Hart, Edicola, 2022
De Goddelijke Formule, Edicola, 2024

In Spanish

El Manuscripto de Ө (Vol 1), El Vidente & La Magdalena, Urano, 2013
El Manuscripto de Ө (Vol 2), El Grial, Urano, 2013

In Russian

Terra Mystica, The Seer, Taripa, 2005

In Korean

The Seer, Inner World Publishing, 2017
The Magdalene, Inner World Publishing, 2018
The Grail, Inner World Publishing, 2019

In Serbian

Iscelitelij (The Seer), Vulkan Izdavastvo, 2012

In Danish

Sjæl I Flammer, Hovedland, 1993
Samsø-digte, Hjortholm, 1994
Zoé, Hovedland, 1995
Skyggerejser, Hovedland, 1998
Hjertets Stilhed, Hovedland, 1999
Den Himmelske Vej, Borgen, 2000
Seeren fra Andalusien, Lindhardt & Ringhof, 2002
Maria Magdalene, Lindhardt & Ringhof, 2004
Gral, Lindhardt & Ringhof, 2006
Det Knuste Hjertes Visdom, Lemuel Books, 2007
Det Aramæiske Mysterium, Lemuel Books, 2008
Frejas Spådom, Lindhardt & Ringhof, 2010
Taxo Luma, Lindhardt & Ringhof, 2012
Terapeuternes Mysterieskole, Gilalai, 2012 (with Githa Ben-David)
Gralstrilogien, Lindhardt & Ringhof, 2012
Lysets Lov, Gilalai, 2013
SHM-Lyset i Mørket, Gilalai, 2015
Seeren, udvidet udgave, Gilalai, 2015
Drengen der gav den blinde sine øjne, Turbine, 2017
Lyset i et Menneskes Hjerte, Harper Collins, 2018
Guds-Formlen, Gilalai, 2020
Lys-Trilogien, Harper Collins, 2020
Vejen, Sandheden og Livet, Eksistensen, 2020
Frihedens Øjeblik, Gilalai, 2021
Daisy – Vi kom svævende, Sacred Seed, 2023
Skæbnespejlet, Sacred Seed, 2023
Det Sande og Det Evige, Alhambra, 2025 (with Naleea Landmann)

In Norwegian

Seeren fra Andalusia, Flux Forlag, 2010
Maria Magdalenam, Flux Forlag, 2012
Gral, Gilalai, 2014

BOOKS BY NALEEA LANDMANN

In English

The Love That You Are – Psalm 119 Meditations, Sacred Seed, 2023
The True and The Eternal, Watkins, 2025 (with Lars Muhl)

In German

Die Liebe Die Du Bist – Psalm 119 Meditationen, Sacred Seed, 2023

In Danish

Den Kærlighed Du Er – Salme 119 Meditationer, Sacred Seed, 2025
Det Sande og Det Evige, Alhambra, 2025 (with Lars Muhl)

BIBLIOGRAPHY

The following books have all meant a world to me. There are so many more, but how many books can you carry?

Aramaic

For those interested in Aramaic I can recommend: *Khaboris Manuscript* by Paul Yonan, *The Hebraic Tongue Restored* by Fabre d'Olivet; *The Poetry of the Lord* by C F Burney; *Aramaic English New Testament* by Andrew Gabriel Roth, *Unconditional Love and Forgiveness* by Edith Stauffer, and all books by George Lamsa, Rocco Errico, Neil Douglas-Klotz and Irene Lipson, to all of whom I am forever grateful.

Yeshua, Essenes, Mariam the Magdalene

Anonymous, *The Gospel of the Holy Twelve*, Watkins, 1950
Audlin, James David, *John the Presbyter*, Volcan Baru, 2015
Audlin, James David, *The Gospel of John*, Volcan Baru, 2013–17
Bock, Emil, *The Three Years*, Floris Books, 1948
Ewing, Upton C, *The Essene Christ*, Philosophical Library, 1961
Furst, Jeffrey, *Edgar Cayce's Story of Jesus*, Neville Spearman, 1968
Griffith-Jones, Robin, *Mary Magdalene, The Woman Jesus Loved*, Canterbury Press, 2008
Larson, Martin A, *The Essene-Christian Faith*, Philosophical Library, 1980

Morgan, C R, *The Gate of Hope*, Pinnacle Books, 1987

Sanderfur, Glenn, *Lives of the Master*, ARE Press, 1988

Schonfield, Hugh, *The Essene Odyssey*, Element Books, 1984

Taylor, Joan E, *Jewish Women Philosophers of First-Century Alexandria*, Oxford, 2003

Taylor, Joan E, *The Essenes, the Scrolls and the Dead Sea*, Oxford, 2012

Telushkin, Joseph, *HILLEL, If not now, when?*, Nextbook, 2010

Trimm, James Scott, *The Book of Enoch – Study Edition*, Worldwide Nazarene Assembly of Elohim, 2005≠17

Welburn, Andrew, *The Beginnings of Christianity*, Floris Books, 1991

Mystic

Amis, Robin, *A Different Christianity*, University of New York Press, 1995

Anonymous, *The Way of a Pilgrim*, Hope Publishing House, 1993

Aradi, Zsolti, *The Book of Miracles*, Longmans Green, 1956

Aurelius, Marcus, *Meditations*, Penguin Classics, 2006

Baha'u'llah, *The Call of the Divine Beloved*, Bahai World Center, 2018

Balsekar, Ramesh S, *A Net of Jewels*, Advaita Press, 1996

Boehme, Jacob, *The Way to Christ*, Paulist Press, 1978

Cayce, Edgar, *A Search for God*, ARE Press, 1942

Chidakarananda and Jayanti, *Meditation on the Imitation of Christ*, Delgado & Olmos, 2013

Damascene, Hieromonk, *CHRIST the Eternal TAO*, Valaam Books, 1999

Evans, Warren Felt, *Esoteric Christianity*, Cornell University Library, 1886

Effendi, Shoghi, *The Dawn-Breakers*, Bahá'i Publishing Trust, 1932

Fuller, Jean Overton, *Noor-un-nisa Inayat Khan*, East-West Publications, 1952

Goldsmith, Joel S, *Practicing the Presence*, Harper & Row, 1958

Greenlees, Duncan, *The Gospel of Hermes*, Theosophical Publishing, 1949

Hodson, Geoffrey, *The Science of Seership*, Rider, 1950

Jinpa, Dorje, *SENSA*, Pentarba Publications, 2012

Johnson, Clive, *The Heart of Loving Kindness*, Labyrinthe Press, 2021

Johnson, David, *A Quaker Prayer Life*, Inner Light Books, 2013

Khan, Hazrat Inayat, *The Complete Sayings*, Sufi Order, 1978

King, Godfré Ray, *The "I AM" Discourses*, Saint Germain Press, 1935

Kovalevsky, Eugraph, *A Method of Prayer for Modern Times*, Praxis, 1993

LeLoup, Jean-Yves, *Being Still*, Paulist Press, 2003

London, Jack, *The Star Rover*, The MacMillan Company, 1963

Mack, John E, *A Prince of Our Disorder – The Life of T E Lawrence*, Little Brown, 1973

Marmion, Columba, *Christ the Life of the Soul*, Sands & Co, 1925

Merton, Thomas, *New Seeds of Contemplation*, Shambhala, 2003

Monroe, Robert A, *Ultimate Journey*, Doubleday, 1994

Muhl, Anita M, *Automatic Writing*, Helix Press, 1963

Nicholson, Reynold A, *RUMI, Poet and Mystic*, Allen & Unwin, 1950

Özelsel, Michaela, *Forty Days*, Threshold Books, 1993

Prophet, Elisabeth Clare, *The Forbidden Mysteries of ENOCH*, Summit Lighthouse Press, 1977

Rambsel, Yacov, *His Name Is Jesus*, Word Publishing, 1999

Roberts, Bernadette, *The Real Christ*, Contemplative Christians, 2017

Schucman, Helen, *A Course in Miracles Combined Volume*, Foundation for Inner Peace, 2007

Schucman, Helen, *The Gifts of God*, Foundation for Inner Peace, 1982

Shantideva, *The Way of the Bodhisattva*, Shambhala, 2008

Skarin, Annalee, *"Ye Are Gods"*, Philosophical Library, 1952

Singh, Huzur Maharaj Sawan, *Philosophy of the Masters 1–5*, Radha Soami Satsang Beas, 1973

Stein, W J, *The Ninth Century and The Grail*, Temple Lodge, 1991

Steiner, Rudolf, *Knowledge of the Higher Worlds*, Rudolf Steiner Press, 1923

Steinsaltz, Adin, *The Thirteen Petalled Rose*, Rowan & Littlefield, 1992

Sunyata, Emmanuel Sørensen, *Dancing with the Void*, Blue Dove Press, 2001

Swedenborg, Emanuel, *Commentary on the Book of EZEKIEL*, New Church Union, 1925

Tillich, Paul, *The Shaking of the Foundations*, MacMillan, 1963

Twain, Mark, *Personal Recollections of Joan of Arc*, Harper & Brothers, 1896

Underhill, Evelyn, *Mysticism*, Methuen, 1942

Wapnick, Kenneth, *Absence from Felicity*, Foundation for A Course in Miracles, 1999

Weil, Simone, *Waiting for God*, Routledge & Kegan Paul, 1951

White Eagle, *Jesus, Teacher and Healer*, White Eagle Trust, 1985

Healing and Health

Apelian, Nicole, and Davis, Claude, *The Lost Book of Herbal Remedies*, Davis, 2021

Bach, Edward, *Heal Thyself*, Saffron Waldon, 1996

Bayne, Murdo McDonald, *Divine Healing of Mind and Body*, Fowler & Co, 1962

Ben-David, Githa, *The Ultimate Book on Vocal Sound Healing*, O Books, 2022

Brofman, Martin, *Anything Can Be Healed*, Findhorn Press, 2003

Cohen, Kenneth S, *Qigong, The Art & Science of Chinese Energy Healing*, Harper, 1997

Eddy, Mary Baker, *Science and Health*, Trustees under the Will of MBE, 1906

Eich, Thomas, *The Work of Bruno Gröning*, Grete Häusler Verlag, 2003

Goldsmith, Joel S, *The Art of Spiritual Healing*, Harper & Row, 1959

Kukor, David E, *The Miracle Oil*, ARE Press, 2008

Sandford, Agnes, *The Healing Light*, MacAlester Park Publishing, 1947

Shelton, Herbert M, *The Science and Fine Arts of Fasting*, Martino Publishing, 2013

Smith, Linda L, *Healing Oils, Healing Hands*, HTSM Press, 2003

Vogel, H C A, *The Nature Doctor*, Mainstream Publishing, 1952

Warner, Felicity, *Soul Midwives*, Hay House, 2013

Weeks, Nora, *The Medical Discoveries of Edward Bach*, C W Daniel Co, 1940

Wolfe, David, *The Sunfood Diet*, Maul Brothers Publishing, 1999

Human Rights

Buber, Martin, *Ich und Du*, Buber Estate, 1923

Douglass, James W, *JFK and the Unspeakable*, Simon & Schuster, 2008

Frankl, Victor, *Man's Search for Meaning*, Rider, 2004

Kennedy, John F, *Let the Word Go – The Speeches, Statements and Writings of JFK*, Laurel, 1988

Kennedy, Maxwell Taylor, *Make Gentle the Life of this World*, Harcourt Brace & Co, 1998

Kennedy, Robert Jr, *The Real Anthony Fauci, Bill Gates, Big Pharma and the Global War on Democracy and Public Health*, Skyhorse Publishing, 2021

King, Martin Luther, *A Gift of Love*, Penguin, 1981

Martin, Joe, *Keeper of the Protocols, The Works of Jens Bjørneboe*, Peter Lang, 1996

Schlesinger, Arthur, *Robert Kennedy and His Times*, Houghton Mifflin, 1978

Schweitzer, Albert, *Reverence for Life*, Harper, 1993

Shiva, Vandana, *Oneness vs the 1%*, New Internationalist, 2019

Encyclopedias and Reference Books

Bhatnagar, R S, *Dimensions of Classical Sufi Thoughts*, East–West Publications, 1984

Bittleston, Adam, *Our Spiritual Companions, Angels, Archangels, Cherubim and Seraphim*, Floris Books, 1980

Burney, C F, *The Poetry of Our Lord*, Oxford, 1925

Cooper, J C, *An Illustrated Encyclopedia of Traditional Symbols*, Thames & Hudson, 1983

D'Olivet, Fabre, *The Hebrew Tongue Restored*, Samuel Weiser, 1921

ESV Study Bible, Crossway, 2011

Fanti and Malfi, *The Shroud of Turin*, Jenny Stanford Publishing, 2020

Fillmore, Charles, *Metaphysical Bible Dictionary*, Unity House, 1931

Green, McKnight and Marshall, *Dictionary of Jesus and the Gospels*, Inner Varsity Press, 1992

Guthrie, Kenneth Sylvian, *The Pythagorean Sourcebook and Library*, Phanes Press, 1987

Hodson, Geoffrey, *Clairvoyant Investigations of Christian Origins and Ceremonial*, St Alban Press, 1977

Jung, Carl Gustav, *Symbols of Transformation*, Routledge & Kegan Paul, 1956

Jung, Carl Gustav, *The Archetypes and the Collective Consciousness*, Routledge & Kegan Paul, 1968

Jung, Carl Gustav, *AION*, Routledge & Kegan Paul, 1968

Kadloubovsky and Palmer, *Writings from the PHILOKALIA on Prayer of the Heart*, Faber & Faber, 1951

Lang, Jovian P, *Dictionary of Liturgy*, Catholic Book Publishing, 1989

Liturgy of the Assyrian Church of the East, Diocese of Australia and New Zealand, 1994

Matthews, John, *The Druid Source Book*, Brockhampton Press, 1998

Mayotte, Ricky Alan, *The Complete Jesus*, Steerforth Press, 1997

Missler, Chuck, *Cosmic Codes*, Koinonia House, 1999

Nicholson and Lee, *The Oxford Book of English Mystical Verse*, Oxford, 1962

Prabhupada, Bhaktivedanta Swami, *Bhagavad Gita as It Is*, The Bhaktavedanta Book Trust, 1983

Robinson, James M, *The Nag Hammadi Library in English*, Brill, 1996

Schipper, Hendrik, *The Messiah Revealed in the Holy Scriptures*, Boaz, 2016

Schonfield, Hugh J, *The Original New Testament*, Firethorn Press, 1984

Stern, David H, *Jewish New Testament*, JNT Publications, 1989

Vanderkam and Flint, *The Meaning of The Dead Sea Scrolls*, Harper, 2002

Vermes, Geza, *The Complete Dead Sea Scrolls in English*, Penguin, 1962

Walker, Barbara G, *The Women's Encyclopedia of Myths and Secrets*, Harper, 1983

WATKINS
1893

The story of Watkins began in 1893, when scholar of esotericism John Watkins founded our bookshop, inspired by the lament of his friend and teacher Madame Blavatsky that there was nowhere in London to buy books on mysticism, occultism or metaphysics. That moment marked the birth of Watkins, soon to become the publisher of many of the leading lights of spiritual literature, including Carl Jung, Rudolf Steiner, Alice Bailey and Chögyam Trungpa.

Today, the passion at Watkins Publishing for vigorous questioning is still resolute. Our stimulating and groundbreaking list ranges from ancient traditions and complementary medicine to the latest ideas about personal development, holistic wellbeing and consciousness exploration. We remain at the cutting edge, committed to publishing books that change lives.

DISCOVER MORE AT:
www.watkinspublishing.com

Read our blog

Watch and listen to
our authors in action

Sign up to
our mailing list

We celebrate conscious, passionate, wise and happy living.
Be part of that community by visiting

f /watkinspublishing   **X** @watkinswisdom
▶ /watkinsbooks   **◻** @watkinswisdom